SEIZE

YOUR

DESTINY

SEIZE YOUR DESTINY

Choices That Lead to a Happy, Successful, and Meaningful Life

George J. Chanos

About the Author

George J. Chanos, Esq. served as Nevada's 31st Attorney General. He administered Nevada's Department of Justice and acted as the state's chief legal officer and advisor. Prior to serving as Nevada's Attorney General, Mr. Chanos had a distinguished legal career, representing individual and corporate clients on all matters relating to the growth and management of their businesses. Mr. Chanos has a common sense approach to dealing with problems and a unique ability to understand and explain complex issues. He also has a clear vision and uncommon insights, concerning how anyone, regardless of circumstance, can design and lead a happy, successful and meaningful life. Mr. Chanos is a father and an uncle. His daughter, Alexandra, is a freshman at Colorado State University, and his nephew, David, is a graduate of San Diego State University. They are both Millenials. They are the inspiration for this book.

For more information on the subjects covered in this book and on related topics, visit gjchanos.com.

To my mother, Marlys Sand, who instilled in me a sense of possibility, a love of beauty, a respect for creativity, an ambition to reach, and the confidence to excel.

To my father, George Chanos, who provided an example of honor and integrity, showed me the dignity of hard work, and taught me the importance of character and family.

Contents

Preface

WHAT LESSONS DO YOU want to leave your children? In November of 2012, I suffered a major heart attack. The experience made me reflect upon my own mortality and sharpened my focus on what's truly important. I realized that there were many important lessons I had yet to share with my daughter and my nephew—both Millennials.

I decided to reduce those lessons to writing to ensure that they would be available to my family in the event that I wasn't there to deliver them personally. This book contains those lessons. In many cases, they are the same lessons that I derived, in large part, from my parents—members of "The Greatest Generation."

As I began reducing my thoughts to writing, I realized that publishing this as a book would advance a broader purpose. It would allow me to make a contribution that might enrich the lives of others—perhaps even entire communities. I offer this book in that spirit and with that hope to readers of all generations.

Life is not easy. Even with the advantages of family, education, employment, and security (things that many of us take for granted), life is full of constant challenges. Without these advantages life can be more difficult than most of us can possibly imagine.

Faced with these challenges, people can lose hope and a sense of direction. They can become fearful, depressed, and paralyzed. They can surrender, lose sight of the importance of personal responsibility, and become frustrated, disillusioned, angry, and dependent. Some look to government to assist people in need, but government is not the answer. Government is inherently inefficient, increasingly dysfunctional, and consistently unreliable. Only by accepting *personal responsibility* for our futures can we lead happy, successful, and meaningful lives.

We need to think about what we want out of life. We need to plan and prepare for what we want, and we need to develop the courage and commitment required to go after what we want. My hope is that this book will assist you and your loved ones in that effort.

One of the most important things that I have learned over my lifetime is that our lives are determined, in large part, by our thoughts.

"Whether you think you can or you can't—you're right" (Henry Ford).

Our thoughts become our words, our words become our actions, our actions become our habits, our habits form our character, and our character becomes our destiny.

Our thoughts influence virtually all of the critical life choices that we make. They impact our level of courage and commitment. They shape our attitudes and perceptions. They affect how we are perceived by others and our relationships with them. Our thoughts influence how we adapt and cope with the challenges that we face. They have an immense impact on our lives and ultimately on our destinies. Our lives begin and end with our thoughts.

You may be thinking, "I can't change, influence, or control my thoughts." Yes, you can, and high achievers do. Your thoughts and your brain are both yours to control. Human behavior is the product of an endless stream of perceptions, feelings and thoughts, at both the conscious and unconscious levels.

The scientific community now recognizes that we have the ability to control our thoughts and to develop our brains in ways never before thought possible. Not only can our brains be improved, they can be influenced and controlled—by us and by others. Chapter 1 discusses how you can control your thoughts by introducing the concepts of neuroplasticity and mindfulness. Chapter 7 discusses the role of our unconscious mind. Chapters 13 and 18 explain how others can influence and control your thoughts by examining the concepts of perception and consumerism.

To lead happy, successful, and meaningful lives, we need to manage our thoughts. We need to develop the courage to overcome our fears. We need to believe in ourselves and recognize the immense potential that exists in each of us. We need to accept personal responsibility for changing the negative conditions in our lives that are holding us back from success. We need to pivot and adapt to changing circumstances and conditions. We need to persevere to overcome the obstacles that we face. We need to make the right choices, and we need to commit to doing whatever is required to achieve our objectives and seize our destinies.

This book will help you to meet and overcome the many challenges that you will face. Its chapters provide detailed discussions of each of the critical concepts, core values, character traits, and skill sets required to successfully negotiate life's challenges. It provides encouragement and direction that can inspire action, build character, and help you overcome your fears. Most importantly, this book explains how learning, accepting, and embracing these concepts, core values, character traits, and skills can empower you, regardless of your circumstances, to overcome the challenges you face. I hope and trust you will enjoy it and profit from it. Action is magic. By reading this book, you are taking the initial action required to seize your destiny. A happy, successful, and meaningful life, as you will soon discover, is available to all of us. Yours is closer and more accessible than you may think.

—George J. Chanos

Introduction

THE TWENTY-FIRST CENTURY MAY ultimately prove to be the most significant century in human history. Those of us who are alive today are witnessing an unprecedented convergence of promise and peril. The opportunities available to Millennials (the roughly 83.1 million people born between 1978 and 1997) in the United States are beyond extraordinary. Some of these opportunities will radically transform life, as we know it.

In 2014, Stephen Hawking said, "Success in creating AI [artificial intelligence] would be the biggest event in human history." Hawking believes that in the coming decades, AI could offer "incalculable benefits and risks." Advances in areas like genomics, biotechnology, nanotechnology, space travel, renewable energy, 3-D printing, cloud computing, and the Internet of Things promise a future unlike anything we can currently comprehend.

The challenges that this generation will face are equally significant. They include political, social, and economic instability and uncertainty; racial, social, and economic inequalities and injustice; environmental threats and resource limitations; cultural and religious tensions; an absence of political accountability, vision, and leadership; and the opportunities and dangers of technology—to name just a few.

As parents, we need to be thinking about the legacy that we will leave our children. Plato once said, "No man should bring children into the world who is unwilling to persevere to the end in their nurture and education." Are you and your children properly prepared for the challenges and opportunities ahead?

Many children clearly are not. There are 17.5 million fatherless children in the United States. There are 1.6 million gang members, who together account for as much as 90 percent of all crimes committed in certain major cities. Half of African-American males and 40 percent of Caucasian males are arrested by the time they are 23 years old. The percentage of children living in low-income families went from 37 percent in 2000 to 45 percent in 2011. Approximately 50 percent of the 6.7 million pregnancies each year in the United States are unplanned.

In many homes, parents are overwhelmed by economic and social challenges. Generational differences between parents and their children, paired with emotional stresses, make communication difficult and at times impossible.

In some homes, parents simply lack the basic parenting skills required to teach their children how to succeed in life. Many parents were never taught those skills by their own parents. Even the best parents acting with the best of intentions are often unable to reach their children for a variety of reasons. Lack of time, ignorance, absence, emotional instability, addictions, poor communication skills, unfortunate circumstances, outside influences and attitudes—the causes are many. In many communities, the focus is simply on survival. Success seems like a foreign concept barely worthy of serious consideration, let alone intense focus and commitment.

Millions of children are never even introduced to or encouraged to embrace the core values, concepts, and skills that lead to happy, successful, and meaningful lives. How then can these young people be expected to make good choices? How can their futures be secure? How can any of our futures be secure if millions of children are growing up without proper guidance?

This book provides an introduction to the core values, concepts, and skills that can assist people in reaching their goals and negotiating the opportunities and challenges ahead and explains how choosing to adopt them can enhance personal and professional relationships, facilitate social and economic growth, and lead to a happier, more successful, and more meaningful life. This book is not a collection of new or novel concepts. Instead, it is a discussion of ancient truths and time-honored values that are as critically important and relevant today as they were when human beings first began to live in groups, tribes, and communities.

Many young people grow up today without the benefit of learning the importance of these truths and time-honored concepts. *This book provides a way to share these life-altering gifts with anyone.*

Convincing young people to sit down and read a book can be difficult. Let that be this book's first lesson—life is difficult. Success requires effort. Those who are unwilling to devote a few hours to read a book that can literally change their lives forever, may not be ready for success.

"Those that will not be counseled cannot be helped" (Benjamin Franklin).

But when they are ready and if they are touched by what they read, then I promise you that the results can be absolutely life changing.

Reading, understanding, and embracing these truths, insights, and concepts will be as relevant and rewarding for parents as it is for their children. It will prove especially useful for parents who are having difficulty communicating with their children. Anyone can profit from reading it. My hope is that this book will transform and enrich entire families.

Aristotle once said, "The man who thinks he knows everything knows nothing at all." I make no claim to know everything. In fact, all I can say with certainty is that there is a great deal I don't know.

This book is not intended as a comprehensive answer to the world's problems. While the values and the teachings it conveys are an absolutely essential part of the answer, simply reading this book will not eliminate your hardships or completely change your life. Only your own actions can do that! But this book will provide the guidance, encouragement, and direction that can inspire transformative, life-changing actions—and taking those actions will change your life.

This book has a very simple yet powerful message. It explains how certain core values and concepts provide the essential foundation for a happy, successful, meaningful life. How we think and how we act influence every aspect of our lives. The twenty-two chapters in this book cover a wide range of subjects. They are intended to inform, enable, and inspire those who want a better life for themselves and their families.

Those who agree with the insights contained in this book are invited to share it with those they care about. Anyone who wants to enhance the happiness and success of another human being should consider sharing the information contained in this book with them. If it enhances the life of even one person, then it was well worth the effort.

One of the most important legacies that we as parents can leave our children is an understanding of and our admonition to embrace the core values that have helped our generation and generations past to meet and overcome all manner of challenges. I can think of no greater gift to leave our children.

CHAPTER ONE

The Importance of Reflection and Self-Examination

Your journey in search of happiness, success, and a meaningful life should begin with reflection and self-examination. This begins with an examination of how we think. Do you control your thoughts, or do you allow your thoughts and the thoughts of others to control you?

What We Know about Neuroplasticity and Mindfulness

According to Jill Bolte Taylor, a Harvard-trained and published neuroanatomist: "Our brain is made up of cells and every ability we have is the product of those cells." Dr. Taylor gave a wonderful TED talk entitled "The Neuroanatomical Transformation of the Teenage Brain." (You can watch it on YouTube at https://www.youtube.com /watch?v=PzT_SBl31-s.)

Previous scientific consensus was that the brain cells you were born with are the same as the brain cells you would die with. The idea was that the brain remains relatively unchangeable over the course of our lives. Scientists no longer believe this to be true. The current scientific consensus is that the human brain is made up of neurocircuitry, which consists of individual connections in the brain that are constantly being removed and recreated, largely dependent on how they are used. This ongoing change in neurons, together with changes in how neurons connect to one another, is called neuroplasticity.

In other words, the brain that you had before you began reading this book is not the same brain that you have now! And it is not the same brain you will have when you're finished reading. You need to think of your brain as a tool. You have the ability to sharpen and improve that tool through reading and learning and through repetition and practice. In fact, every experience you have will change the connections in and the performance of your brain. The human mind, both conscious and unconscious, still holds enormous mystery. A great deal of our everyday experiences are controlled by our unconscious mind and happen outside of our awareness. However, we now know that we have the ability to influence the development of the unconscious mind and even overrule unconscious impulses through conscious decisions. We also know that the prefrontal cortex is responsible for planning and orchestrating our thoughts and actions in accordance with our goals and integrating our conscious thoughts, perceptions, and emotions. In sum, we know that we have the ability to learn. We have the ability to increase our IQs. We have the ability to improve both our conscious and unconscious minds, and we have the ability to master a wide variety of skills. The question is—what are we doing with these incredible abilities?

Malcolm Gladwell studied the lives of extremely successful people to find out how they achieved success. In the book *Outliers*, Gladwell says that it takes roughly ten thousand hours of practice to achieve mastery in a field. Repetition and practice alter the connections in your brain and have a profound impact on your abilities and your performance.

In the March 2016 issue of *Esquire*, Kareem Abdul-Jabbar quotes Bruce Lee as saying that he was not concerned about someone who had practiced 10,000 kicks. He was more concerned about a person who had practiced one kick 10,000 times. Abdul-Jabbar says, "I was that person. That's why the hook was such a formidable weapon."

By 1962, the Beatles were playing eight hours per night, seven nights per week. By 1964, the year they burst onto the international scene, the Beatles had played more than 1,200 concerts together—more than most bands will play in a lifetime. At his peak, Tiger Woods worked an average of twelve hours a day, from 6:30 a.m. to 7 p.m. If he was not practicing, he was playing; if he was not playing, he was weight training; if he was not weight training, he was reading, watching film, or thinking about how to further improve his game. All of these physical and mental activities impacted the connections in his brain and his performance.

Bolte Taylor also says, "*We are capable of mindfulness. We are capable of changing our thoughts and changing our brains. We have the ability to pick and choose what's going on inside our heads.*"

Mindfulness is a state of active, open attention to the present moment. When you're mindful, you observe your thoughts and feelings more consciously. Instead of letting your life pass you by, mindfulness means living in the moment and awakening to all types of experiences, thereby allowing for increased recognition of mental events in the present moment. Mindfulness is the essence of engagement. When we are living in the present, in the moment, we are less likely to plague ourselves with fears about the future or regrets about the past. By paying attention to what's happening around us instead of operating on autopilot, we can reduce stress, unlock creativity, and improve our performance. We also become more alert to opportunities.

We all rely very heavily on our unconscious thoughts, we have to, our unconscious thoughts are required to process the 11 million bits of information that impact all of our brains every second. We rely on our unconscious minds to handle our sensory perception, our memory recall, and most of our routine everyday decisions. Some scientists estimate that we are conscious of only about 5 percent of our cognitive function. The other 95 percent happens outside our awareness. That being said, we not only have the ability to control our conscious thoughts, through controlling our conscious thoughts, we have the ability to influence, develop and control many of our unconscious thoughts and impulses. Successful people operate on a different level than most people. They focus more intently. Those who perform at the highest levels are the most focused—the most mindful. They develop and improve their minds and their ability to perform at a higher level. They read—some veraciously. They practice—some relentlessly. They exercise control over their conscious thoughts and through their positive thoughts and activities they are able influence and impact the development, nature and control of their unconscious thoughts and impulses. In sum, they use and develop their conscious and unconscious brains.

If you're a parent, you remember the joy and excitement that your children experienced when they tasted their first strawberry, saw their first puppy, or looked up and saw white clouds drifting across a bright blue sky. That excitement came from being naturally mindful. We are all still surrounded by life's natural wonders. The gravity of these incredible experiences hasn't changed. What has changed is our appreciation of them. In her book *The Little Book of Mindfulness*, Patrizia Collard says, *"By reconnecting with these simple moments in life, by truly living moment by moment, it is possible to rediscover a sense of peace and enjoyment. We may, at least sometimes, feel once again truly enchanted by life."*

When we start to focus on positive thoughts, we let go of our fears and anxieties. We become more joyful and less stressed. We perform at a higher level. Even focusing on things that are painful can be beneficial by preventing us from staying in a bad relationship and helping us to understand and overcome our depression or anger. Collard talks about how mindfulness can facilitate acceptance that leads to healing. She offers the example of Buddha telling the story of the "two arrows" to his visitors:

> Life often shoots an arrow at you and wounds you. However, by not accepting what has happened, by worrying about it, by saying it was unfair and wondering how long the pain will last, we tend to shoot a second arrow into the open wound and increase and prolong the pain. Pain is often a given, but suffering is optional.

Bay area pain specialist Michael Moskowitz injured his neck in a waterskiing accident. He tried everything to relieve his debilitating pain—rehab, drugs, rest, nothing worked. Eventually, he turned to mindfulness. He looked at images of his brain's pain center firing. He then imagined shutting that pain signal off. He did this over and over again. He also forced himself to concentrate on positive mental tasks. He focused on reading, writing, and working. He forced himself to concentrate on his work and ignore the pain. Eventually, his brain rewired itself to focus on the positive tasks and stopped sending pain signals.

People who are struggling with weight problems can use mindfulness to control their weight. Imagine eating a raisin very slowly, while contemplating and appreciating everything about it: the smell, the texture, how it looks, the taste. By practicing mindfulness while eating, we can cultivate an appreciation for the food we have and develop a sense of well-being that eliminates our emotional cravings.

In sum, there is growing evidence that we do, in fact, have the ability to control our thoughts. We do this by experiencing life more fully, more consciously, and more mindfully as it unfolds. It is important that you understand this critical concept. You have the ability to control your thoughts and you need to use that ability. Learning to control your thoughts is an ongoing process that requires focus and effort. You won't gain control over your thoughts immediately and your level of control will never be total or absolute, but with effort, focus and mindfulness, greater control over your thoughts is absolutely possible. By controlling your thoughts, you can develop the courage to overcome your fears. You will gain greater capacity and an increased willingness to believe in yourself and recognize your immense human potential. You will begin accepting personal responsibility for changing your condition. You will learn how to pivot and adapt to changing circumstances. You will recognize the need to push forward and persevere to overcome the challenges that you face. You will begin to think about all of your choices more carefully and make only the right choices. You will focus and commit, to doing that which is required to achieve your objectives and seize your destiny. All of this begins and ends with your thoughts. You have the ability to develop and improve both your conscious and unconscious mind through reading, experience and practice and you have the ability to gain greater control over your thoughts through focus, positive affirmation and mindfulness.

Who Are You, and Who Do You Want To Be?

Ask yourself the following questions:

+ Who am I?

+ How do I perceive myself?

+ How do others perceive me?

+ How do I want to be perceived?

+ What are my strengths and weaknesses?

- What do I want to do with my one and only life?
- How do I intend to get there?

After reading this book, you will be in a much better position to engage in the kind of self-examination and reflection required to answer these questions. Once you finish the book, asking and answering these questions should be your first step.

Self-examination and reflection are important because we all need to take inventory of ourselves to determine our strengths and weaknesses. Once you understand your strengths, you can seek opportunities that allow you to leverage those strengths. Understanding your weaknesses will allow you to minimize disappointments and focus on areas in need of improvement.

People are unique. We all have distinct strengths and weaknesses. Not all generalizations about any group or generation apply equally to all of its members. That being said, some groups do share certain characteristics.

The Millennial Generation

"Millennials" or "The Entitlement Generation" may be the most misunderstood and maligned generation in history. They have a generally, although not universally, accepted reputation of being arrogant, lazy, and self-centered. If you're a Millennial, you don't even like being called a Millennial. Why would you? Millennials have been subjected to a seemingly endless stream of criticism.

If you're a Millennial, it is important that you understand where this criticism is coming from and the motives behind that criticism. When it's coming from your parents and your grandparents, it's coming from those who love you and want only the best for you. We believe in you! We recognize your amazing strengths—along with your weaknesses. We understand that you are different than we are, in many respects, and we embrace and applaud many of those differences. We are incredibly proud of you. If we didn't care about you, we wouldn't question your decisions. We wouldn't challenge you. We wouldn't waste our time offering you our advice. We recognize that we can learn from you as much if not more than you can learn from us. We simply want to help.

As a parent and a grandparent, nothing is more important to us than you are. As you contemplate criticism, it is important that you consider the source and the motivation behind the criticism. When the source is your family – the motivation is love. Your employers are also parents and grand parents. They have children just like you. They see the same issues with their children that they see with you – and they genuinely want the same things for you that they want for their own children. They want you to succeed. They want to help you! Your employers are also motivated to help you out of economic self-interest. The more successful you are, the more they benefit. If you are receiving feedback or criticism from either your family or your employer, it is because they genuinely want to help you succeed. Remember that.

Millennials have been characterized, rightly or wrongly, as having a delusional sense of entitlement. As evidence of millennials' self-absorption and narcissism, some have commented on their continuously updated Facebook profiles and their obsession with selfies. Certain studies even support this conclusion. While there may be some support for this conclusion, it should be noted that Millennials are also the most networked and connected generation in history. Updating their digital profiles, texting, and posting images are important parts of how they stay connected. All of this is called networking, and Millennials are better at it than any prior generation.

The Pew Research Center's reports on Millennials reveal a highly intelligent, complex generation that is technologically advanced and globally oriented. Millennials have been taught to value individuality and see themselves as independent thinkers. They are not defined by their jobs. Instead, they want to define their jobs. Most have no interest in working in a cubicle. They believe that advances in technology and mobility should allow them to work anywhere with a Wi-Fi connection. This generation is the most educated workforce ever. They have high expectations. They do not want to stay at jobs they find unfulfilling.

The Brooking's Institution reported, "Almost sixty-four percent of Millennials said they would rather make $40,000 a year at a job they love than $100,000 a year at a job they think is boring."

Millennial workers are the first generation to question work as a priority. In contrast with prior generations, they place quality of life first and work second. They believe in working smarter, not harder. This generation uses technology to multitask and to find shortcuts to accomplishing tasks. Advances in technology and the ubiquitous nature of technology have created the potential for millennial workers to be more competent and efficient than any prior generation.

What emerges is a complex generation that appears to have what every generation and every individual has—significant strengths and weaknesses. In 2015, Millennials became the largest generation in the U.S. labor force. At Pricewaterhouse Coopers, 4 out of 5 workers in 2016 will be Millennials. Millennials can benefit from understanding the discussions surrounding their purported strengths and weaknesses. It will help them to determine whether or not certain descriptions may apply to them. This self-examination will also help them to understand how their parents, grandparents, and prospective employers may perceive their behavior. Learning more about prior generations will give Millennials important insights into the mindsets and perspectives of their elders and prospective employers.

What Do We Know about Prior Generations?

Members of "the Greatest Generation" grew up during the Great Depression. They watched their parents lose their homes, their businesses, and their jobs. Then, just as the economy at home had begun to recover, World War II broke out in Europe and Asia.

Members of the Greatest Generation went from their high school graduations to distant places like Iwo Jima and Normandy to fight against two of the most powerful and ruthless military machines ever assembled, Germany and Japan. They faced incredible odds with honor and dignity. They succeeded on every level. They literally saved the world as we know it. If you're a Millennial, these are your grandparents.

After World War II, they came home and immediately began rebuilding their lives. Having grown up in the Great Depression, this group was primarily concerned about economic security. They married in record numbers and gave birth to another distinctive generation, "the Baby Boomers," born between 1946 and 1964. If you're a Millennial, the Baby Boomers are your parents. I was born in 1958. I'm a Baby Boomer.

More of the Greatest Generation attended college than any prior generation. They were responsible for major breakthroughs in science and technology. They gave the world new art, literature, and industry. The Greatest Generation wanted their children to have better lives than they had, so Baby Boomers were raised to work hard, pursue traditional careers, and save their money. Baby Boomers were taught that if they worked hard, they could thrive and prosper.

The seventies, eighties, and nineties represented a time of unprecedented prosperity in the United States. Baby Boomers did even better than expected. This left them feeling optimistic. Baby Boomers generally had more positive life experiences than their parents. They instilled in their millennial children a feeling that they were somehow "special" or "gifted." In the eighties and nineties, the prevailing child-rearing philosophy was that building a child's "self-esteem" was of utmost importance. Parents tended to praise children constantly and not recognize one child's achievements as superior to another's.

According to some studies, the Boomers' child-rearing practices resulted in an increase in narcissism and a sense of entitlement among their offspring. In studies that measured psychological entitlement and narcissism, millennial respondents scored 30 percent higher on the Narcissistic Personality Inventory than Baby Boomers, placing Millennials in the "highly entitled" range. Others have challenged these findings, suggesting that what some see as narcissism may actually just be increased self-confidence. Clinical psychologist Joseph Burgo writes that true self-confidence grows out of "behaving in ways that you respect by meeting your own standards." Narcissists, by contrast, have exaggerated or even delusional perceptions of themselves. Their actions betray their inflated self-concepts. The University of New Hampshire's Associate Professor of Management Paul Harvey says, "Narcissists believe they're special or faultless but often lack any real justification for the belief."

You may recognize some of these traits in yourself or your friends. Parents, you may see some of these traits in yourself or your children—or you may not. This is why taking inventory of your own strengths and weaknesses is important. By understanding yourself better, you can leverage your strengths and modify or protect against your weaknesses.

The Danger of Delusional Beliefs and a Sense of Entitlement

Delusional beliefs and a sense of entitlement are two incredibly destructive forces. Either one can prevent you from ever becoming successful or realizing your dreams. An incident involving Cho Hyun-ah, the privileged daughter of Korean Air's chief executive Cho Yang-Ho, illustrates how delusional beliefs and a sense of entitlement can be incredibly destructive forces. Cho Hyun-ah was head of flight services for her father's airline.

Ms. Cho was a passenger on Korean Air when a flight attendant served her nuts in a bag (not on a plate). She ordered the pilot to go back to the terminal at New York's JFK airport to offload the attendant, who was fired on the spot, before she allowed the plane to resume its journey. Ms. Cho was later charged with violating aviation safety laws for impeding a flight crew in their duties. Her father, Chairman Cho Yang-Ho, apologized for his daughter's "foolish act." Ms. Cho was required to step down from her job. She also faced a possible three-year prison term for violating aviation safety laws.

Clearly, Ms. Cho suffered from the delusional belief that her desire to make a point outweighed all competing considerations. After all, as the daughter of the chairman and the head of flight service, surely she was entitled. She was wrong.

The choices of a 23-year-old student named Charlie provide yet another example of behavior based on a delusional sense of entitlement. Charlie is not from a privileged family. While attending college in San Diego, Charlie decided, over the objections of his family, to move to the beach. While he lived there, his grades declined, and he collected ten parking tickets, which he ignored. When his father asked him how he could get and ignore ten parking tickets, his response was, "There's nowhere to park at the beach." Charlie ignored the second part of the question dealing with why he ignored the ten parking tickets. His father's wise response was to ignore Charlie's need for a car. He demanded that the car, which he had purchased for Charlie, be returned, he then sold the car to pay off his son's parking tickets.

The loss of his car forced Charlie to have to move away from the beach so that he could walk to work and classes. His father felt that the lesson (choices have consequences) would be of greater value to Charlie than the car. His father was right. The idea that Charlie would think that the absence of a parking space allowed him to park wherever he wished, and then ignore the resulting parking tickets, evidenced a delusional sense of entitlement.

Attitudes like these will always have negative consequences, whether you're the daughter of a billionaire, like Ms. Cho, or the son of a middle-class father, like Charlie. This sense of entitlement is not limited to the privileged or to Millennials whose parents may have spoiled them. Many people have a delusional sense of entitlement. Rather than accept personal responsibility, they think that someone else is responsible for them, or they think that rules don't apply to them. We see it everywhere: people who cut in line, people who take more than their fair share, people who run red lights, those who expect or demand accommodation or assistance, and those who fail to show gratitude for the help they do receive—all of these people suffer from a sense of entitlement.

We see the same sense of entitlement in certain privileged and intelligent Millennials who operate under the false assumption that intelligence somehow guarantees success. They see their intelligent, successful parents and conclude that because they, too, are intelligent, they will automatically be successful. What they don't seem to understand is how hard their parents have had to work for their success. Perhaps that's because much of their parents' hard work occurred before they were born or while they were too young to notice. Or perhaps their sense of entitlement comes from how they were raised. While the cause of their miscalculation may be uncertain, the flaw in their logic is undeniable. Intelligence alone does not guarantee success. Intelligence + hard work + core values (generally) = Success. Even then, there is no guarantee.

We see a similar sense of entitlement in those Millennials who believe that they are somehow entitled to the respect of others, including, but not limited to their parents, teachers, employers, and even the police. Some expect and demand respect even though they offer little respect in return. What they fail to understand is that respect cannot simply be demanded—it must be earned. The idea that we are somehow entitled to the respect of others, regardless of our own actions, is a false assumption. We are not. No one owes any of us anything—least of all his or her respect. We must earn the respect of others through our own positive actions.

These irrational and destructive mindsets are not reserved to Millennials. They are exhibited and adversely affect people of all ages. If you suffer from either delusional beliefs or a sense of entitlement and if you don't resolve to get past these maladies, you will, without question, increase your likelihood of failure.

Decide Who You Are and Who You Want to Be

The important question is who are you? How do these descriptions apply to you? How do you perceive yourself? How do others perceive you? How do you want to be perceived? Who do you want to be?

How you dress, your grooming, your posture, your eye contact, your demeanor, your attitude, your handshake, your table manners, how you speak, your phone manner, the format of your resume, the way you phrase a letter, your presence on social media, your views on social and political issues—all affect the impression you make on others. Think about how you may be perceived by others and about how you want to be perceived. Then work with patience, humility, and dedication toward meriting the perception that you want and believe you deserve.

Regardless of what generation you come from, if you think your special—Stop! You're not. Regardless of what technological skills you may possess or how smart you think you are, you will not succeed without hard work, commitment, perseverance, and a fidelity to core values. If you want to be respected, show respect for others—earn their respect.

You have the ability to control your thoughts. Who you are is determined by how you think, act, perceive yourself, and how others perceive you. Decide who you want to be, and then work toward becoming that person.

Life is a continuous journey of self-improvement. Begin by realistically assessing your personal strengths and weaknesses. Think about what you want to achieve and how your strengths may be leveraged to advance those objectives. Consider how your weaknesses may impact your objectives and how you can address, mitigate, or improve upon those weaknesses. Then begin to move forward toward realizing your goals and objectives. Taking such actions will eventually increase your likelihood of success. Action is magic. Every journey begins with a first step. Design yourself as you would design a temple. One carefully laid and thoughtfully considered brick at a time.

CHAPTER TWO
An Early Fork in the Road:
Conformity v. Nonconformity

S UCCESS IS OFTEN DEFINED as getting what you want out of life or attaining your goals. Learning how to succeed in any society begins with understanding the nature of that society. Societies are generally defined as people living together in organized communities with shared laws, traditions, and values. People who understand and embrace these shared laws, traditions and values are more likely to flourish in such societies. They are more likely to obtain employment, stay out of trouble, and lead productive lives.

Conversely, people who ignore or reject these shared laws, traditions, and values are less likely to succeed. Accepting these principles can be an important part, if not a prerequisite, to leading a happy, successful, and meaningful life. This raises a number of issues relating to conformity, individualism, artistic expression, and choice.

Many people see nonconformists as troublemakers. People who challenge generally accepted beliefs are often perceived as a threat. Yet it is undeniable that nonconformists have been essential to many of the greatest advances in human history. Many of the world's greatest discoveries and achievements would never have been possible without courageous nonconformists. Despite this, nonconformity can be a risky proposition. Challenging the status quo often meets with significant resistance. Moreover, there are different types of nonconformity and different reasons for nonconformity. There are also varying degrees of nonconformity—and degrees matter.

Enlightened Nonconformity

In *Zero to One*, by Peter Thiel and Blake Masters, Thiel (co-founder of PayPal and an enlightened nonconformist) says that whenever he interviews someone for a job, he likes to ask this question: *"What important truth do very few people agree with you on?"*

Thiel is looking for people who have the capacity to see possibilities that do not yet exist. He is looking for brilliant and enlightened nonconformists, and he is right to do so. Why? He knows that these are the people who change the world.

Thiel is not interested in hiring conformists who are satisfied with the status quo or even people who want to incrementally improve upon that which already exists. He doesn't want to hire people who see a candle and want to make and sell thousands of candles. He wants to hire that rare individual who sees a candle and imagines a light bulb, or better yet, a light source that heats and cools the home.

Thiel points to increased global development, pollution, and consumption and warns that in a world of scarce and limited resources continued growth without new technology is unsustainable. "Only by imagining and creating new technologies," says Thiel, "can we make the 21st Century more peaceful and prosperous than the 20th." Thiel is looking for the enlightened nonconformists who can imagine and create those new technologies. Most of the greatest advances and developments in human history have been imagined and created by visionaries who saw something no one else did and decided to do something no one else was doing.

Historic examples of enlightened nonconformity include the following:

+ The printing press (Johannes Gutenberg)
+ The steam turbine (Charles Parsons)
+ The light bulb and moving pictures (Thomas Edison)
+ The airplane (Orville and Wilber Wright)
+ Wireless telegraphy (Guglielmo Marconi)
+ The gasoline-powered automobile (Gottlieb Daimler)
+ The computer (Alan Turing and Konrad Zuse)

Modern examples of enlightened nonconformists include the following:

+ Ted Turner (CNN)
+ Steve Jobs (Apple)
+ Bill Gates (Microsoft)
+ Elon Musk (SpaceX and Tesla)
+ Larry Page and Sergey Brin (Google)
+ Mark Zuckerberg (Facebook)

Principled Nonconformity

Principled nonconformity can be a wonderful choice if your nonconformity is based on sound, rational principles and serves a noble or positive purpose. In some cases, it can be the only correct choice. Standing up for an idea or a principle that you believe in, even if your view is not widely accepted, may be an appropriate or even a necessary act of nonconformity. If you are standing up for what is true, right, or just, then challenging the status quo is more than defensible. It's honorable.

The political arena is in desperate need of principled nonconformists. Having served as Nevada's attorney general, I had an opportunity to witness politics firsthand. I didn't like what I saw, and I see very serious problems for the country ahead. In my opinion, today's political environment is more toxic and dysfunctional than it has ever been. The system is broken, and it will take principled nonconformity to create any real and sustainable change.

The nature of our species is to evolve and adapt. The current system, in which the public interest is being subverted by corporate special interests, is unsustainable. Our system must evolve into something more responsive to its constituencies, or those constituencies will adapt. Adaptation could either take the form of continued complacency, or it could eventually result in revolution. Given the nature of Millennials and the tools available to them, I believe that continued complacency is unlikely.

In 2004, Arianna Huffington wrote *Pigs at the Trough: How Corporate Greed and Political Corruption Are Undermining America*. In it, she details how politicians have continued to be complicit in facilitating massive transfers of wealth from taxpayers to corporate special interests. The pigs have been feeding at the trough ever since, and they will continue to eat us out of house and home until principled nonconformists rise up and stop them.

Boeing is the second largest federal contractor in the United States. Despite making $5.9 billion in profits in 2013, Boeing received a tax refund/credit of $199 million. This is a company that depends on taxpayer money for over 30 percent of its business yet consistently contributes little, if anything, in taxes to pay down the federal deficit or balance the federal budget. Over the past dozen years, during which Boeing reported a total profit of more than $43 billion, the company's net cumulative refund of federal taxes has been more than $1.6 billion.

The United States is the only major nation in the world that has passed legislation prohibiting the government from negotiating drug prices. That's right, your elected representatives actually passed legislation, as part of Medicare Part D, prohibiting Medicare from negotiating the prices that Medicare pays for drugs, allowing drug companies to reap their greatest profits from the American market and American consumers/taxpayers. Canadians pay a fraction of the costs that Americans pay for the very same drugs. That alone is unacceptable. But it gets worse.

"The pharmaceutical lobbyists wrote the bill," says Congressman Walter Jones (R-NC). "The bill was over 1,000 pages. And it got to the members of the House that morning, and we voted for it at about three o'clock in the morning."

Why would your elected representatives allow a vote on a one-thousand-page bill of this magnitude to come to the floor for a vote at three o'clock in the morning? To avoid media coverage. To hide it from you!

The pharmaceutical industry spent hundreds of millions of dollars, lobbying state and federal elected officials laying the groundwork for legislation that was passed under cover of media darkness—legislation that has facilitated billions of dollars in taxpayer-funded profits to the pharmaceutical industry.

How can this happen without an outpouring of national outrage? Why are any of the elected representatives who voted for this bill still in office?

Incredibly, Pfizer, which played a major role in supporting and lobbying for this legislation and profits immensely from this legislation, is in the process of changing its own tax domicile to Ireland. Pfizer has already sheltered $74 billion by holding it overseas and declaring that the money will remain abroad "indefinitely." More importantly, our elected representatives have allowed all of this to happen. Large corporations and their lobbyists have created loopholes enabling corporations to avoid an estimated $100 billion per year in taxes by shifting profits to the Cayman Islands and other offshore tax havens. This is obscene! These elected representatives work for us. They are our employees.

Members of Congress owe us a fiduciary duty, the highest duty of fidelity known under the law—yet they are allowing us all to be robbed and our natural resources to be raped by corporate special interests that are making financial contributions to their campaigns. It's patently outrageous and should be illegal! In my opinion, this is either gross malfeasance or outright fraud against the American taxpayer. This is our current political system. Not very good, is it?

Boeing and Pfizer are just the tip of the iceberg. Corporate tax breaks now exceed $100 billion annually. In January of 2013, the Fiscal Cliff Bill provided Goldman Sachs with $1.6 billion in tax-free financing for its new headquarters through Liberty Bonds. Why on earth should taxpayers be subsidizing the new headquarters for one of the world's most successful private investment banking firms?

Today, 99 percent of all new income in the United States is going to the top 1 percent, while the top one-tenth of 1 percent own almost as much wealth as the bottom 40 percent. In the last two years, the wealthiest 14 people in this country have increased their wealth by $157 billion. That increase is more than is owned by the bottom 130 million Americans—combined. That bears repeating. In the last two years, the wealthiest 14 people in this country have increased their wealth by $157 billion. That increase is more than is owned by the bottom 130 million Americans—combined. This increase is astonishing! Even more significant is the fact that our system of government, the system that is supposed to represent all 320 million Americans, is actively involved in facilitating that massive transfer of wealth. This is not merely astonishing—it's disgusting. You don't need to be a progressive, a liberal or a moderate to understand or agree that this is obscene. Even conservatives who believe in a free market can recognize the inherent inequity of such massive transfers of wealth and the obvious injustice of a rigged game. One can admire the qualities of capitalism while still abhorring the actions of cheaters and the perils political patronage and preference. Money in politics perverts and distorts capitalism to a degree that makes it both unrecognizable and unattractive. It creates undue influence and inherent unfairness. The independent voices, on both ends of the political spectrum, are now beginning to respond to this inequity and injustice. People who never had any involvement in politics are beginning to rise up and voice their discontent. This issue transcends political parties and is beginning to attract independents to candidates who, in prior elections, wouldn't have attracted significant followings. The Bernie Sanders campaign and the Donald Trump campaign are the two most obvious examples of this phenomenon. The degree to which we allow money to influence our political system is central to who we are and who we want to be as a nation, and it will only become more significant over time. The people of this country have had enough, and many of them are beginning to act upon their discontent. More will follow.

People like Lawrence Lessig, professor at Harvard Law School, formerly a professor at Stanford Law School, are leading the charge for campaign finance reform in an effort to stem the influence of money in politics. Lessig is a principled nonconformist. He is a board member of MAPLight.org, a nonprofit research group focused on illuminating the connection between money and politics. In his 2011 book, *Republic Lost: How Money Corrupts Congress—and a Plan to Stop It*, Lessig offers a manifesto for change. His focus is on the core problem of corruption in both political parties and their elections. Change Congress, the Fix Congress First project, and the Rootstrikers project were all created to help volunteers address the problem of money in politics.

Examples of principled nonconformists include the following:

+ Thomas Jefferson (one of the Founding Fathers and third U.S. president)

+ Abraham Lincoln (sixteenth U.S. president)

+ Mahatma Gandhi (leader of the Indian independence movement)

+ Nelson Mandela (former president of South Africa)

+ Anwar Sadat (former president of Egypt)

+ Benazir Bhutto (former prime minister of Pakistan)

Principled nonconformity, when based on what is true, right, and just, is a beautiful choice.

Personal Nonconformity

Personal or stylistic nonconformity raises a variety of discrete issues that need to be considered in determining whether it represents a good or a bad choice. A little bit of personal or stylistic nonconformity can be a good thing. You want some degree of individuality. It makes you more interesting. It makes you—you. The questions are, how far should you take it, and why are you doing it?

Some believe that conforming to certain shared laws, traditions, and/or values offends their sense of individualism or inhibits their artistic freedom. They may, therefore, choose not to adopt or conform to society's shared norms. This is a choice. For some, this may even be the right choice, a choice that leads to a happy, fulfilling life. Individuals who find success or happiness through their nonconformity may simply be people who value their nonconforming lifestyles over other more traditional goals or objectives. If these individuals are willing to risk sacrificing those traditional goals or objectives in order to maintain a nonconforming lifestyle, or if someone's lifestyle advances his or her own goals and objectives, then nonconformity may be the right choice for them.

For those who have traditional goals and objectives and hope to pursue them through traditional channels, a nonconforming lifestyle may be a poor choice. Moreover, if your nonconformity is purely stylistic, emotionally or irrationally based, or if it is done out of frustration or anger with no real purpose or meaning, then it can be an extremely limiting or even a destructive choice. We need to understand that people's views evolve and are subject to change. This is especially true with young people. Therefore, certain personal or stylistic acts of nonconformity that can have long-term consequences are often very poor choices.

People change: What you want today may be very different from what you want tomorrow. According to the Pew Research Center, 40 percent of Millennials already have at least one tattoo. I hate to be the bearer of bad news, and I fully expect that some may disagree with me, but in my view, for people who are under 25, that's not a great choice. Here's why. Let me begin with one simple observation. The prefrontal cortex of the brain, which is responsible for our rational, conscious thought, does not fully develop until we are 25 years old. This alone, should be sufficient reason for everyone to delay making a permanent or even a semi-permanent change to their bodies—until they are at least 25.

What you want when you are 16 or 18 is rarely what you want when you are 25 or 30. Yet, some decisions are difficult, if not impossible, to change. For example, young people who are attracted to a nonconforming lifestyle when they are teenagers may get tattoos and/or piercings. That might be a great look when you're younger. It may even make some young people more popular in high school or college, leading them to believe they've made the right choices.

At that age, you may think that you are willing to sacrifice all or most of life's more traditional goals and objectives in the name of nonconformity. You may have no interest in working in a traditional career. Or you may have given up on the idea of pursuing a traditional career—perhaps because you believe a traditional career is beyond your potential or simply doesn't interest you. Think again. After high school or college, you are likely to have a different outlook on life. At 25 or 30, you might decide you want to pursue some of life's more traditional careers. As you get older, more mature, and more confident, your thoughts, opinions, and goals are certain to change. What looked highly unlikely at 18 may seem far more reasonable and achievable at 25. You may even decide that you want a career in one of the more traditional fields, like law or finance, where tattoos and piercings may place you at a disadvantage or foreclose opportunities. You may end up wanting a job in high-commission sales or at a high-end retailer or hotel, where tattoos may limit your options. Why limit yourself? Ask yourself a simple question—"Is getting a tattoo or a piercing really worth limiting my options in life?"

Annually, thousands of people attempt to remove tattoos that they acquired when they were younger. According to the American Society for Aesthetic Plastic Surgery, 45,224 procedures for tattoo removal were performed in the United States in 2014. Almost three-quarters of them were performed on women. More than half of laser removals last year were for individuals between 19 and 34 years old. Preferences change. People change. Unfortunately, tattoos are permanent. They don't change. That makes them a risky choice and often a poor choice.

Not all generalizations apply with equal force to all individuals or groups. You may be part of a culture, community, group, or profession where tattoos are common. Artists, musicians, and athletes often fall into this category. Everyone you know may have them, and you may conclude that getting a tattoo is not only justified—it's advantageous. You may be right. In your culture, community, group, or profession, tattoos may not hold you back. They may even help you thrive or survive. But once you venture outside of that culture or profession, your tattoos may be more of a liability than an asset. You need to assess and weigh these competing considerations. In my view, outside of nontraditional or artistic callings, tattoos generally limit rather than expand people's options, and that is rarely a good thing. The important point is that you give all important decisions serious thought—nowhere is this truer than with permanent or semi permanent decisions. As noted above, this advice is especially true for people under 25 whose views, opinions, needs, wants, and attitudes are subject to constant and major change. If your over 25, make your own decisions on what's right for you.

The same is true of certain postings on the Internet. Today, many kids are posting photos and information on the Internet that they are likely to regret later. Some post nude, risqué, or compromising photos. Others post obscene or inappropriate messages. These postings may make you more popular with some of your peers, but they can also become a permanent record of your poor judgment, searchable by any prospective admissions officer, employer, future business partner, or prosecutor. This makes such postings exceedingly poor choices.

In Paterson, New Jersey, a first grade teacher was dismissed for posting comments about her students on Facebook. One comment read, "I'm not a teacher. I'm a warden for future criminals."

In Saugas, California, two teens were arrested for posting nude photos. If anyone sends or posts nude photos of underage kids, such actions are considered to be child pornography, which can carry an eight-year prison term. Very bad idea!

The kinds of material that teens are posting on the Internet today is beyond reckless. In some cases, these choices are beyond comprehension. What have you posted? Parents—what have your children posted?

Finding Clarity among Mixed Messages

One reason that this can all seem very confusing, is that society sends us mixed messages about nonconformity. We see successful nonconformists everywhere we look. They're the charismatic agents of change in business and politics. They're successful celebrities on TV, in music and film, on billboards, and in magazines. Why wouldn't anyone want to be a nonconformist?

Again, nonconformity is not always the wrong choice. It may be the right choice for those individuals whose nonconformity is embraced by society and facilitates, rather than frustrates, the attainment of their goals and objectives. Even personal and stylistic nonconformity can sometimes aid rather than impede success. Examples of this are often found in the performing arts, where a successful artist's or musician's nonconforming style is admired by society and actually contributes to the attainment of that individual's goals.

Certain performers, like Lil Wayne and Snoop Dogg, have an edgy counter-culture style that actually contributes to their successes. This illustrates how personal and stylistic nonconformity can, in rare instances, be the right choice for some people. However, these examples can be extremely misleading and cause others to make poor choices. The type of personal or stylistic nonconformity exhibited by certain performers and celebrities will rarely be the right choice for most of us.

Why is this true? It's true because what society accepts from highly talented performers like Lil Wayne is far less likely to be considered acceptable behavior outside the performance environment. Without his talent and work ethic, Lil Wayne's personal and stylistic nonconformity would make him virtually unemployable in many more traditional fields. The same is true for Snoop Dogg or anyone who exhibits that degree of stylistic nonconformity. Without their rare talents, their stylistic nonconformity would limit rather than increase their options. This is true despite the fact that these are intelligent and driven men.

You also need to realize that most of the values discussed in this book are no less essential to the success of these artists than they are in any other field of human endeavor.

Lil Wayne has been quoted as saying, "All I am is music. That's all I do and all I know, 365 days a year, twenty-five hours a day, eight days a week. This is my life and what I breathe. It's who I am." Wayne goes on to say, "I work hard everyday. Hard work is everything. How do I know, because I work hard."

Do you know how Lil Wayne got his start? When he was 11 years old, he met Bryan "Baby" Williams and Ronald "Slim" Williams, the founders of Cash Money records. He kept beeping them until they finally said, "Come up to the office." There was nothing for him to do at the office, so he sat down and wrote rap lyrics. He would go to school, do his homework, get straight As, and then hang out at Cash Money Records writing raps. He did this for a full year before they finally handed him a microphone. They recorded him at age 12. The rest is history. That's how Lil Wayne got his start. His work ethic is every bit as intense as Tiger Woods,' and like Tiger Woods, he's been that way since he was a child. If you want to be like Lil Wayne, you better be prepared to work like Lil Wayne.

Nicki Minaj, the first female artist Wayne signed to his Young Money label says, "He taught me the true meaning of work ethic. Even when you're the boss, work like it's your first day on the job."

These two artists are regarded as nonconformists. Yet their comments make it clear that their successes are just as dependent on the values discussed in this book as are the successes of individuals pursuing more traditional careers. In other words, even those who adopt a nonconforming personal or stylistic lifestyle must embrace certain core values to succeed. Success requires it. It's not optional. It's not dependent on circumstance. It's mandatory. For those who choose to emulate the nonconforming stylistic choices or lifestyles of these artists without attaining some measure of societal acceptance and/or commercial success, nonconformity will be a poor choice—a choice that can lead to failure, unemployment, isolation, and depression.

There are varying degrees of nonconformity. While having a sense of style and exhibiting creativity may actually improve your chances of success in certain fields, if done excessively, they can be a liability. Employers want to hire people who will enhance, not undermine, the opportunity for their businesses to be successful. The quality of their lives depends on it. Their families depend on it. Therefore, it helps if you consider the perspectives of potential employers before making certain decisions about the nature and degree of your personal or stylistic nonconformity. In deciding what level of nonconformity is right for you, be purposeful, thoughtful, and measured. Think ahead.

CHAPTER THREE

What Do You Want to Do with Your One and Only Life?

I**F SUCCESS IS** "GETTING what you want," then you first need to decide what you want out of life. Life is not easy. On the contrary, life is very difficult. But for those who want more out of life and are willing to do what is required to achieve their goals, the possibilities are endless.

Fulfilling your potential requires intense drive, determination, and commitment. It requires taking personal responsibility for your success and doing all that is required to achieve your objectives. Success is not reserved for the privileged few. It is available to anyone who is willing to do that which is required to achieve his or her goals.

Most, if not all of us, want more out of life, but we lack the courage to believe in ourselves enough to go after what we want. Others, who may have the courage to try, lack the intense desire, determination, and commitment required to achieve their objectives. We don't try hard enough. We give up. We settle.

The genius and the greatness of America has always been and continues to be the fact that America places no limits on what any man or woman can achieve.

Everyone is burdened by various circumstances, mental and/or physical limitations or conditions—some more than others. Life isn't fair or easy. Regardless of the obstacles we may need to overcome, we are all capable of improving our lives. We are limited only by our own desires, abilities, and determination. Moreover, we live in an era where our options for transforming our lives are virtually unlimited.

Financial success, if that's what you want, is available to anyone who has the desire, ability, and determination to acquire it. Neither family connections nor even an education are required to accumulate wealth. Countless rags to riches stories attest to this fact. Andrew Carnegie, the father of the global steel industry, was born into poverty. He immigrated to the United States when he was a child—with no formal education. He built an empire worth around $300 billion (adjusted for inflation), making him four times richer than the richest man alive today.

However, success isn't just about money. It's about creating and leading a life that you can look back upon with a feeling of pride, satisfaction, and fulfillment.

When he delivered the commencement speech at Stanford University in 2005, Steve Jobs told the graduates:

> Your time is limited, so don't waste it living someone else's life .... Don't let the noise of other people's opinions drown out your own inner voice. Most importantly, have the courage to follow your heart and intuition. They somehow already know what you truly want to become.

Jobs encouraged the graduates to do what they love and to keep looking until they find it. He repeatedly told them: "Don't settle."

Success doesn't just come to us. We need to go after it. Opportunity comes to all of us in one form or another. But we need to be ready for it. We need to recognize it, we need to seize it, and we need to make the most of it.

Your choices are as varied as the human personality. The twenty-first century is the first century in human history that allows individuals to leverage their connections to other individuals via the Internet. This generation has the ability to create careers and businesses that have never even existed before. What will you do?

Creating New Technology

Mary Barra, CEO of General Motors Company, says,

> Just like they did when I was starting out, the STEM fields provide some of the most rewarding careers in America today. As engineers, scientists, and inventors, we get to imagine what's next, and then make it happen.

Steve Jobs, Apple's cofounder said, "I think everybody in this country should learn how to program a computer because it teaches you how to think." Coding isn't nearly as difficult as you may think. It's not easy, or everyone would be doing it. But if you have an aptitude for math or science, computer technology may be the perfect field for you. You can learn to create and execute your own programs on your laptop or smartphone in a matter of weeks. You can also spend a lifetime learning more and perfecting your craft. It could provide you with an amazing and rewarding career. An experienced software developer can earn over $100,000 a year. More important, when combined with creative and original thought, it can open up entirely new worlds.

Google began in March 1998 as a research project by Larry Page and Sergey Brin, doctoral students at Stanford University. With more than 300 million monthly active users, it is now one of the most important and successful companies in the world. Google's 2014 revenue was $18.1 billion. As of December 31, 2014, Google had $64.4 billion worth of cash, cash equivalents, and marketable securities.

Mark Zuckerberg founded Facebook with his college roommate and fellow Harvard University student Eduardo Saverin. It launched in February of 2004. The website's membership was initially limited by the founders to Harvard students but was expanded to other colleges in the Boston area, the Ivy League universities, and gradually most universities in Canada and the United States. By September 2006, it was open to everyone 13 years of age and older with a valid email address. In 2014, Facebook had over 1.35 billion monthly active users and posted $12.466 billion in revenue.

Palmer Luckey started ModRetro, an online forum, for gamers and hackers to come together to help each other modify their game consoles. When he was 18, he built a head-mounted gaming display because he couldn't find one he liked. When he was 20, he raised $2.4 million on Kickstarter to fund Oculus Rift, and when he was 21, he sold it to Facebook for $2 billion.

Ayah Bdeir, the founder of littleBits (www.littlebits.com), started taking programming lessons at age 12. Today, her company, which sells miniature electronic building blocks that snap together magnetically, is doing business in more than seventy countries.

If you are interested in coding, many different free options to learn how to code are available online. You can take 100-percent free, online introductory computer science courses from Harvard (Course CS50, at www.edx.org) or Stanford (Course CS101, at www.cousera.com). These are the same courses that some of the greatest minds in the country have taken, and they are available to you—today—for free! What are you waiting for?

CodeAcademy (www.codecademy.com) is another option. On its interactive website, you can learn to code in HTML/CSS, Javascript, PHP, Python, and Ruby on Rails by building and executing your own code projects. The release of CodeAcademy's Hour of Code app for iPhone has made it even easier to learn the basics of coding. This app teaches users to code and run their first program in less than an hour on their iPhones. CodeAcademy's project-based learning programs are also 100-percent free.

Code.org (www.code.org), an initiative backed by Facebook, Google, and Apple, also offers a number of free beginner's tutorials for learning how to code. Hopscotch (www.gethopscotch.com), a build your own games app, allows anyone—kids or adults—to build and share an original game. In Hopscotch's first year, users have produced and published more than one million original games.

Becoming an Online Sensation

At age 24, United Kingdom online sensation Zoe Sugg has 2.6 million followers on Twitter. Her beauty, fashion, and self-help videos on YouTube have been watched more than 400 million times. Her first novel, *Girl Online*, sold 78,000 copies in its first week of publication—more than any previous debut novel on record in the UK.

Brandon Stanton, a 30-year-old former bond trader, created the popular blog, "Humans of New York." Mr. Stanton takes pictures of ordinary people and interviews them about their lives. Published in book form, Humans of New York became a number-one best seller.

A young Frenchman named Jerome Jarre came to the United States with less than $500 to his name. Using nothing but his phone and his imagination, he began posting Vines and Snapchats of his random, humorous encounters with complete strangers. His posts became viral sensations. He now has more than eight million followers and one billion views. He has done Vines with Pharrell Williams and Ashton Kutcher. Brands now pay him $25,000 per Vine video. He has a new Snapchat show supported by Robert De Niro, and he is reported to have turned down $1 million dollars to endorse an unhealthy food product. Not bad for a kid who came to this country with nothing but imagination, determination, and a great personality.

Twenty-one-year old Marques Brownlee (aka MKBHD) has been called "the best tech reviewer on the planet." This YouTube phenom has more than 2.3 million viewers. He began uploading tech reviews while still in high school.

There are currently more than one billion smartphone users. Apps like Periscope and Meerkat are being used to create live videos that are quickly and easily broadcast on Twitter, Facebook, and YouTube.

Internet sensation Josh Paler Lin did a YouTube video entitled, "How does a homeless man spend $100?" It generated over 28 million views on YouTube. In the video, Josh gives a homeless man named Thomas $100 and then follows him to see how he spends it. He documented how the man used the $100 to buy food for other homeless people. Josh then leveraged the video to start an Indiegogo campaign, which raised over $120,000 for Thomas.

YouTube is the world's second-largest search engine. It draws millions of viewers who watch creative videos showing everything you can imagine. Advertisers and sponsors want to capture those viewers. Google bought YouTube in 2006 and holds regular workshops for promising YouTubers to help them create content and grow their brands. The deal is, you generate original content and get half of the ad revenues your videos attract. The bigger the audience you can build, the more money you and YouTube stand to make.

Eight years ago, Corey Vidal was just another wanna-be YouTuber, working in his parents' basement with a camera, recording one dance video after another and posting them on YouTube. His online obsession caused tension at home. He moved out and ended up in a homeless shelter. All he had was his computer and an idea: to lip synch a song with a Star Wars theme. Crazy, right?

He performed it, filmed it, and posted it. In the first day, his video got thirty thousand views. The next day it got 100,000 views, and then YouTube ended up featuring it on its Canadian homepage. His video then went viral, getting millions of views. Vidal now has a dozen full-time staff. With two hundred thousand subscribers on his two YouTube channels, Vidal has a steady audience and a steady income stream. He says, "We've made millions off of YouTube." If you have creative talent, this could be you. Think of things that you're good at, for example:

- Something you do better than any of your friends
- Something you have a real interest in doing
- Something other people might want to learn more about
- Something people might just like to watch
- Something funny, educational, useful, unusual, interesting, or entertaining

What kind of video might you be able to create that other people would want to watch?

Getting Discovered Online

You've heard of Justin Bieber. At 17, he was discovered on YouTube by former So So Def marketing executive Scooter Braun and eventually signed to Usher's Raymond Braun Media Group.

In early 2015, soul singer Leon Bridges was washing dishes for a living in Fort Worth, Texas. He uploaded a song on SoundCloud that quickly went viral. Record labels got into a bidding war over signing him. After signing with Columbia, he released his debut album, "Coming Home," in June of 2015. Since then he has been on a global tour.

You may be an aspiring young artist. You may dream of becoming the next Lil Wayne, Pharrell Williams, Iggy Azalea, or Drake. You may love and admire their styles, strengths, lifestyles, or successes. You may want to be just like them. That's understandable. You're not alone. Tens of millions feel the same way. It is possible. Others have done it. But before you move in that direction, it is important that you understand something: The odds of anyone becoming a successful recording artist are extremely low.

That doesn't mean you shouldn't try. On the contrary, if this is what you want, it means you need to do more than try. It means you need to be relentlessly committed to the pursuit of your dream. If you want to be like Lil Wayne or any of these artists, then you need to approach your career like they do: 366 days a year, twenty-five hours a day, eight days a week. If you have talent and make the required effort, it can happen. It is possible.

Although anything is possible, you also need to be realistic. At some point, it should become clear to you whether you have the truly rare gifts required to achieve your objective. If you do, then keep trying. Try harder. Do everything you can to make your dream a reality. However, if and when you come to realize that you don't have those exceedingly rare gifts, or your gifts are not quite at that level, then the best advice anyone can give you may be to simply accept that reality and change direction.

Don't take too long figuring this out. As soon as you become convinced that things are not going to work out moving in one direction, you need to change course and move in a more promising direction. The keys are to be realistic, objective, and flexible.

Do knowledgeable and objective third parties confirm that you have what it takes? Do the responses that you are receiving through social media and other artist platforms confirm that you are on the right track? Are you truly committed to doing what it takes to succeed? If the answer to these questions is yes—then go for it! Be relentless in the pursuit of your dream.

On the other hand, if you're just living out a fantasy that has no basis in reality, or you are not relentlessly driven and committed, then move on. Living on false hope isn't really living. It's pretending. Children pretend, and you're no longer a child.

In the meantime, preserve your options. Don't do anything that would limit you from later switching directions and pursuing other paths. It would therefore probably be wise to hold off on the tattoos and piercings until after you sign with your first label. That way, you'll maximize your available alternative options if a change in direction becomes necessary or appropriate.

If you're an aspiring artist, you don't need to rely on agents or promoters to be discovered. YouTube (www.youtube.com) allows creative talent to take their talents directly to consumers and generate revenue or get discovered.

TuneGo (www.tunego.com) is a music discovery platform that allows new talent to be discovered by the music industry. ADD52 (www.add52.com) is another music-discovery platform, built in conjunction with the digital agency All Def Digital, cofounded by Russell Simmons.

Urban Indie Radio (www.UrbanIndieRadio.com) is an independent, royalty paying radio station in Los Angeles that promotes independent music. TalentHouse (www.talenthouse.com) provides unknown artists with an opportunity to work with big bands, musicians, and other established talents on projects through an open call for submissions.

If you're a painter, sculptor, graphic designer, or visual artist, ArtDiscover (www.artdiscover.com); Behance (www.behance.net); and DeviantArt (www.deviantart.com) are online platforms that allow contemporary artists from around the globe to be discovered.

If you're a writer, www.specscout.com allows aspiring screenwriters to showcase their talents to the film industry without the need for an agent. Not one of these opportunities was available to prior generations, but they are all available to you!

Becoming an Entrepreneur

T. J. Johnson, at age 29, cofounded a consumer drone startup called AirDroids, developed a rough prototype of a drone, and put it on Kickstarter. He and his partners hoped to raise $35,000. They ended up raising $929,212 in just sixty days. Preorders on the AirDroids site exceeded $1.2 million.

The website One Red Paperclip was created by Canadian blogger Kyle MacDonald, who bartered his way from a single red paper clip to a house in a series of fourteen online trades over the course of a year. Kyle has now turned that website into a creative marketing agency.

The most successful entrepreneurs are typically highly creative and intensely determined. They are also risk takers. According to Rodney "Mutt" Mullen, "Real innovation and grit comes from loving the process." Mullen revolutionized the world of skateboarding as a teen. He was intensely driven. He won thirty-four of the thirty-five contests he entered during his Hall of Fame career. He invented tricks that had never been done before by anyone. He later became a partner in World Industries, a skateboard manufacturer, where he designed and patented a skateboard truck that significantly improved board handling and performance. When a private equity firm acquired World Industries, Mullen became a multimillionaire.

When injuries from skating made it difficult for him to walk, let alone skate, Mullen turned his attention to mastering Linux. He poured over how-to manuals and attended Linux user forums. He learned everything he could. The more he learned about Linux, the more he saw parallels between how hackers craft code and how skaters invent tricks. Both involve using a trial-and-error process to sequence small bits of information into coherent wholes. Street skaters begin by mastering physical tricks and then have to figure out how to pair those tricks with fixed objects in the urban landscape.

Mullen also noticed that a willingness to fail was essential to innovation. Skaters must endure the physical pain of falling dozens of times each day. Mullen believes that skaters who embrace the transformative nature of failure are the only ones capable of attaining greatness. Mullen made his speaking debut at TEDxUSC with the talk entitled "Pop an Ollie and Innovate." He is now one of the most sought-after speakers on innovation.

Think Outside the Box

In a Stanford master of business administration (MBA) class, students were split into teams. Each team was given $5 and told to use it to make as much money as possible in one week. At the end of the week, each team would be given 10 minutes to make a presentation to the class about its approach. Teams tried various approaches, ranging from gambling to making and then selling restaurant reservations to people standing in line at popular restaurants. The winning team was even more creative than the rest. They sold their 10-minute presentation slot to a small company that used it to get in front of the class of Stanford MBA students.

Creativity is about thinking outside the box. It's about challenging assumptions. It's about doing something others haven't done. It's about discovering or developing a new path to improvement. Uber is the world's largest car service, but it owns no cars. Alibaba is the world's most valuable retailer, but it holds no inventory. Airbnb is the world's largest provider of accommodations, but it owns no real estate. In each instance, these companies' creators found ingenious new ways to rethink and redesign old business models.

Others are even bolder and more ambitious. Companies like Planetary Resources, backed by the likes of Larry Page and Eric Schmidt of Google, are already launching satellites to scan asteroids for space mining opportunities. Planetary Resources values the nickel, iron, cobalt and other materials that make up an asteroid called Davida, at more than $100 trillion. That's more than five times the GDP of the United States. Mining a speeding asteroid, something that few would consider possible and even fewer would attempt, is thinking way outside the box.

We Live in an Age of Unlimited Resources

Companies like Kickstarter and Indiegogo allow aspiring entrepreneurs to crowdsource and crowdfund new business models and ideas online. Go to Kickstarter (www.kickstarter.com) and Indiegogo (www.indiegogo.com) to see the thousands of entrepreneurs who are starting creative new businesses.

A company called AngelList (www.angellist.com) also provides funding for new businesses by connecting institutional and angel investors to early stage start-ups. Never before has there been greater, more democratized access to capital. Technology now provides access to information and resources that did not exist in prior generations.

Alcoa's CEO, Klaus Kleinfeld, describes 3D printing as "the second Industrial Revolution" or "production at your fingertips." A production process that once took six months and cost tens of thousands of dollars can now be completed in two to eight weeks at a fraction of the cost.

You don't have to rent space and open a storefront to start a business. You can merely open your laptop and create an online business to design, produce, or sell virtually anything. You also don't necessarily need a factory to manufacture what you design. In some cases, you can manufacture the products you design in your home on a 3D printer. These changes in access to capital, technology, and distribution provide unprecedented opportunities for creativity, independence, mobility, and prosperity. Use them to create something new and useful.

Becoming a successful entrepreneur can be one of the most satisfying and rewarding things anyone can do. You will work harder than you ever have, but if it's right for you, you will love every minute of it.

The KISS Principle

It is also important to note that entrepreneurship isn't reserved for creative geniuses or limited to revolutionary ideas. Ray Kroc, the legendary founder of McDonald's, built his fast food empire around the KISS Principle—"Keep It Simple, Stupid." Some people waste years trying to find the perfect idea. They think of ideas that are complicated, difficult to execute, or capital intensive. Ideas, for the most part, are a dime a dozen. Everybody has one. Sometimes the simplest ideas, ideas that you can actually execute, are the best ideas. You can find books that are filled with good business ideas, any one of which can make you money. That's just a starting point. What takes something from an idea to money in the bank? Action and execution.

Here's an extremely simple idea; it's about as simple as they get. In the right hands, this idea could make someone rich. It requires little if any education, little if any training, and minimal capital. It simply requires the right person to see it, love it, and work it.

Virtually all retail locations have windows. Shop owners typically pay a minimum of $20 to have their windows washed. It takes approximately twenty minutes to wash the windows of a standard retail location. That's the equivalent of $60 per hour. Assume you were to pursue this opportunity and you were the only one working. You might wash ten windows a day. That's $200 a day. What if you hired ten people to help you and paid each of them $10 per window? That's $30 per working hour for them and $10 profit per window for you. If each of your ten workers did ten windows a day, that's $100 for each worker per day and $100 x ten workers or $1,000 in profit, per day, for you. Only the number of shops you could sign up and the number of workers you could keep busy would limit the amount of money you could make.

This is a business that virtually anyone could start with less than $100. All you need is a bucket, water, soap, a squeegee, clean rags, a six-foot ladder, friends who need jobs, and the ability to walk into a store and sell them on your service. Once you sell one business, if you do good work, others would follow. With each job you are given, you would ask the owner whether he or she would like you to come by once a week or once every other week. Before you know it, you will have built a network of clients and a busy schedule. You will have started your own business.

People all over the country start businesses just like this every day. Some wash windows, some walk dogs, some do landscaping, some clean pools, some sell cold bottles of water on hot summer days, some shovel snow. These are the jobs that virtually anyone can start at a very early age.

When I was 10 years old, I had a snow shoveling business. I would go door to door and ask homeowners to pay me $5 to shovel the snow off their driveways. People loved it. Who wants to go out in the cold and shovel their own driveway when they can pay an enterprising kid $5 to do it? I would hire my two younger cousins to help me shovel and pay them $1 each. That gave me a $3 profit per driveway. I had more money than any other 10-year-old I knew. Today, an enterprising kid could probably get $20 or more per driveway. Have two friends help you and pay them $5 each. That would leave you with a $10 profit for each driveway. Not a bad gig for a 10-year-old.

Entrepreneurship is simply finding a good or service that people are willing to pay for and then delivering that good or service at a profit. That's the essence of capitalism. There is nothing quite like it.

Becoming a Professional Athlete

Attempting to become a professional athlete is a very low-probability endeavor. You may want to play professional sports, but unless you possess the rare physical gifts of a professional athlete and the intense commitment required to become a professional athlete, it's simply not going to happen. Deluding yourself into thinking that it will happen is going to reduce, rather than increase, your chances of having a happy, successful, and meaningful life.

Parents and young adults need to realistically evaluate athletic prospects and consult with coaches. If someone realistically has high-level potential, then by all means, the development of his or her athletic talents and skills should be encouraged. On the other hand, if a person is not an exceptional athlete, then perhaps making more time for academics or developing a trade skill would be a better option.

Many parents encourage their children to get involved in sports. If this is to teach a child the many benefits of athleticism, it's a great choice. If it is to explore the possibilities of a career in coaching, physical training, or other athletic endeavors, this may be a great choice and direction. However, if this is being done to push a child toward a career in professional sports, this may prove to be a poor choice for all but the select few who have the natural ability and intense drive required of collegiate or professional athletes. In any case, athletics should never be a substitute for academics. Mental agility will always prove more valuable than physical agility in negotiating life's challenges.

Athleticism should be a significant part of everyone's life. It encourages a healthy lifestyle and builds discipline, a strong work ethic, and self-esteem. Participating in athletics promotes cooperation, commitment, and teamwork. But it should not be all consuming. Parents often encourage a child's interest in sports or accept their natural gravitation toward sports. It may seem like a logical choice. The child likes it, athleticism has many natural benefits, and the coaches are good role models and caretakers. It may seem to work for the whole family. However, you and your parents also need to think ahead. What happens after high school when collegiate or professional sports are no longer an option? What happens when you can't get into college because you can't pass a college entrance exam? What happens when you can't get a job because of your poor reading and math skills? Is that what you want? If not, then you may need to reassess the logic of certain choices. You need to think ahead and keep your options open.

Again, if you have the rare physical gifts of a professional athlete and the intense commitment required to become a professional athlete, then by all means, go for it! However, if your skills are not truly extraordinary, or you lack the intense drive, determination, and commitment required, then you need to consider and explore other options.

Consider Doing Something Extraordinary

There is no greater measure of success in life than helping others. Numerous important issues could benefit from your skills and dedication. Mark Twain once described the universal brotherhood of man, as "our greatest possession." Horace Mann once said, "Be ashamed to die until you have won some victory for humanity."

Think about issues that interest and concern you. Then think about how you may be able to help bring about the solutions required by those issues. Don't be alarmed by the many significant issues facing America and the world—and don't ignore them. Understand them and strive to play a meaningful role in addressing them. Many people run away from problems. Leaders have the courage to run toward problems and fix them. Control your destiny. Be part of the solution.

Political dysfunction may be the most important and pressing issue facing America today. Virtually all major issues are impacted by politics. In 430 B.C., Pericles said, "Just because you don't take an interest in politics doesn't mean politics won't take an interest in you." Today's political environment is more paralyzed and dysfunctional than at any point in my lifetime. Americans' current confidence in Congress is not only the lowest on record, but also the lowest Gallup has recorded for any institution in the forty-one-year history of the poll. This is also the first time Gallup has ever measured confidence in a major U.S. institution in the single digits. Currently, only 4 percent of Americans say they have a great deal of confidence in Congress, and only 3 percent have quite a lot of confidence. About one-third of Americans report having "some" confidence, while half have "very little," and another 7 percent volunteer that they have "none." Special interests have a stranglehold on politicians in both parties. At a time when the country needs "principled nonconformists" and "enlightened statesmen," the halls of Congress are littered with ideologues, egotists, opportunists, and those who are simply unqualified to act upon the tasks at hand. America is adrift—like a ship without an anchor. We lack clear and comprehensive policies concerning issues like immigration reform, gun ownership, the proper role of law enforcement, and America's foreign policy direction. We need our elected representatives to engage in a search for the "best" solutions. Instead, our elected representatives have been unable to offer any comprehensive solutions, let alone the "best" solutions.

Society has become increasingly polarized. Highly partisan constituencies monopolize and polarize the public debate, while the "silent majority" of Americans are too preoccupied with the challenges of daily life and too disillusioned by the political dysfunction they see to even participate in the debate, let alone forcefully advocate their more rational centrist views. Media, which attempts to secure a defined and captive market share by appealing to politically segmented audiences, reinforces ideological and political divides. According to a survey by the Pew Research Center for the People & the Press, over the last ten years, virtually every news organization or program has seen its credibility marks decline. Today, only two news organizations—*Fox News* and local TV news— receive positive believability ratings from at least two-thirds of Republicans. A decade ago, only two news organizations did not get positive ratings from at least two-thirds of Republicans. By contrast, Democrats generally rate the believability of news organizations positively—with the exception of *Fox News*. Why do Democrats generally rate the believability of news organizations positively? Because the media has done a good job of targeting and appealing to Democrats. Millennials, who are mostly Democrats, represent the largest and most significant emerging demographic market—larger than the Baby Boomers. Advertisers want to reach Millennials. Consequently, some media programing specifically targets Millennials by appealing to their liberal biases. Just as *Fox News* targets conservatives by appealing to their conservative biases. This is why media credibility ratings continue to plummet. The real question is should any of us, including Millennials, trust media organizations, liberal or conservative, that intentionally target, reinforce and appeal to our biases? Is that what we really want and need from our news organizations? Gerrymandering of congressional districts (the act of manipulating district boundaries to create partisan-advantaged districts) has caused elected representatives on both sides of the aisle to focus on pandering to their partisan constituencies in order to secure their own reelection. Running in highly partisan districts designed to ensure their reelection, members of Congress have little if any incentive to reach across the aisle to find better, more comprehensive solutions. To do so, they fear, might actually work against their own reelection. The influence of money and special interests over both individual candidates and party leadership causes many elected representatives to disregard the needs of the country and focus instead on their reelection and/or advancing the interests of their party.

The world is becoming more dangerous, and America has become more polarized and paralyzed. We simply don't have the luxury to continue suffering this incompetence and malfeasance.

Iran, with the support of Russia, and North Korea, with the support of China, have become increasingly antagonistic. Russia, faced with declining oil prices and a deteriorating economy, has become increasingly nationalistic and aggressive. The proliferation and possible use of nuclear weapons and/or highly radioactive material, remain enormous threats with unstable countries like North Korea and Iran becoming increasingly provocative and unpredictable. Vladimir Putin, intent on restoring the grandeur of imperial Russia has expanded its reach in Ukraine and Syria, increasing tensions in the region and making a clash with NATO member Turkey more likely. China has built up and reclaimed an archipelago of man-made islands, now spanning 2,900 acres, in the South China Sea. U.S. officials fear the islands, built in international waters, will be used for military purposes and may pose a threat to one of the world's biggest commercial shipping routes. In February of 2016, China stationed anti-aircraft missiles on the disputed islands. You will hear much more about this issue in the future. Both Russia and China engage in daily cyber attacks against American interests; Islamic extremists are using encryption technology (which was originally designed to protect America's data and communications from being compromised) to inspire lone-wolf attacks against America and its allies. Perhaps most disturbingly, at the same time that Islamic extremists are actively attempting to solicit recruits for a global jihad, domestic divisions over religious, ethnic, and racial lines have caused America to become more divided than at any time since the Civil Rights movement—creating a potentially rich recruiting ground within our borders for jihadists. Syria's civil war has created the worst humanitarian crisis since the end of WWII, causing displaced Syrian refugees to seek asylum in Europe and America, with the threat of Islamic terrorists infiltrating their ranks.

In February of 2016, James Clapper, Obama's director of national intelligence, told the Senate Armed Services Committee that we now face, "the most diverse array of challenges and threats that I can ever recall." In sum, our threats have multiplied while political competency and accountability in this country have diminished. Call me alarmist, but to me, the convergence of increased danger and diminished competency creates legitimate cause for concern.

America's foreign and domestic policies need to be reexamined. Many of our current approaches to major foreign policy and domestic issues are simply not working. America will confront risks regardless of what policy is adopted. No direction eliminates risk. The correct policy is one that will minimize those risks. Republicans advocate peace through strength. Democrats advocate peace through restraint. Both approaches are incomplete solutions, and neither approach has thus far proved effective.

Neither carpet-bombing nor isolationism will solve the problem of radical Islamic terrorism. This problem is multidimensional and nuanced. It is also becoming increasingly urgent. No one has offered a thoughtful and comprehensive strategy for dealing with the problem, and the current approach is clearly not working. The threat of radical Islamic terrorism cannot be assessed and addressed simply by reference to its current form, scope, or breadth. This is a profoundly dangerous and rapidly growing movement that, if allowed to do so, will only become larger and more threatening over time. It must be defeated *before* it gains further strength and momentum.

Finding the correct approach to all of the issues that we face as a nation will require that we rethink our overall strategy. It will require major structural changes in how we govern ourselves. Implementing and executing on any approach will present even greater challenges. As a country, we need to come together and try to reach consensus on what policies will most effectively reduce America's long-term risks and increase our long-term security. We then need to execute on that plan. We need to do this not as a divided and fearful country, unsure of our direction and purpose, but as a united and courageous country, firm in our commitment to one another and resolute in our determination to protect our families and our homeland. We are not doing this today. We are not united. Instead, we are deeply divided. Why? Ideology, partisanship, ego, money, and fear. The tragedy is that solving imminent problems and devising effective strategies should not be about Republicans or Democrats. Finding the right solutions, to protect our national security, should not be about ideology, partisanship, ego, or money, and we cannot afford to be paralyzed by fear. All elected federal representatives, regardless of party, regardless of what state or congressional district they may be from, have a fiduciary duty to all Americans—to do what is right for all Americans. In no area is this more important than in the areas of national defense and national security.

Winston Churchill once said, "Sometimes it is not enough that we do our best, sometimes we must do that which is required." What is required here is that we focus on our shared interests and put our individual and party interests aside. National defense and national security are too important to be driven by simplistic ideologies. The stakes are far too high for politicians and the media to be manipulating public opinion over critical issues, simply to draw contrasts between political parties during a presidential campaign. The country doesn't need more contrast. It needs more cooperation. Americans will recognize and follow the right plan. They simply need to be presented with the right plan. Our elected representatives should be working together to develop, build consensus around and execute on that plan. The media should be assisting in that effort by focusing on areas of agreement rather than exacerbating conflict.

Instead, politicians are focused on retaining or regaining their political power during a presidential election, while media organizations are focused on increasing ratings and market share by fanning the flames of conflict and appealing to their ideologically segmented audiences. It is important that we elect the right person as president in 2016, but it is equally important that we move forward after the election, united in purpose and supportive of the "best" plan possible.

Some may regard what we are seeing today as "business as usual." That may be true, but these are far from usual times. It is not enough to rely on the fact that America is "the most powerful nation in the world". That meant something when Teddy Roosevelt was president, but it means far less today. For better or worse, we have entered an era of profound change; an era in which wars can be waged on a laptop and the power of great military forces can easily be circumvented; an era in which those who wish to harm America are successfully using social media to recruit and inspire Americans, yes Americans, to commit lone-wolf attacks and other acts of treason; an era in which encrypted communications make detecting and preventing attacks by such actors more difficult and at times impossible; an era in which "business as usual" has become increasingly dangerous. We can no longer afford to accept "business as usual" from our elected representatives. Extreme polarization and intense political dysfunction cannot be allowed to become "the new normal." The need to reform and repair our government, the need for campaign finance reform, the need for "citizen statesmen" and "principled nonconformists," and the need for unity and cooperation will only become more urgent over time.

How might you be able to help? Begin by understanding that things can and should be better. Expect and demand more from your elected officials and the media. Understand the issues and demand the fundamental and structural changes that this nation so desperately requires. Demand an end to the corrupting influence of money in politics. Demand an end to gerrymandering. Question your assumptions. Be alert and informed. Consider all viewpoints from a diverse mix of media outlets, especially those that help you question your assumptions, before arriving at conclusions. Be open and flexible. Be willing to compromise. Be thoughtful and courageous. Listen and learn. Get involved. Vote. Organize. Lead.

Global warming, a term used to describe a gradual increase in the average temperature of the Earth's atmosphere and its oceans, is likely to be a major issue for this and future generations. Many believe that global warming is leading to permanent changes in the Earth's climate. There is still significant debate over the ultimate impact of global warming, but most climate scientists, looking at the data and facts, agree that the planet is in fact warming, that humans are the primary cause, and that this phenomenon may have significant adverse consequences for the planet. Changes resulting from global warming may include rising sea levels due to the melting of the polar ice caps, as well as an increase in the occurrence and severity of storms and other severe weather events. Many believe this to be one of the most important issues facing our planet. Others disagree. They argue that the science surrounding the likely impact of climate change is uncertain and that restrictions on energy production will do more harm than good.

Secretary of State John Kerry, speaking at the U.N. Climate Summit in Paris, also known as COP21, said,

> I don't, frankly, look to government to solve this problem. It's the private sector, the next Elon Musk or Steve Jobs is going to find a way to do battery storage for alternative and renewable energy, or we're going to find a way to burn energy, or maybe this dream of fusion is going to be accelerated and actually have a commercial viability. I don't know the answer, but I have absolute confidence in the ability of capital to move where the signal of the marketplace says "go" after Paris.

Are you the next Elon Musk or Steve Jobs? How can you make a difference?

Look for the insurance industry to become move active in the global warming debate. The number of weather-related events covered by insurance has tripled since the 1980s, and the cost has jumped from $10 billion annually to some $50 billion. Learn more about the issues, and reach your own conclusions.

Water is likely to be a major issue in your future. Willem Buiter, Citigroup's chief economist, says, "Water as an asset class will, in my view, become eventually the single most important physical-commodity based asset class, dwarfing oil, copper, agricultural commodities and precious metals." Access to clean water ought to be a human right, but as global populations continue to grow, waste and misuse of this precious resource may challenge that assumption. Desalination plants, grey-water recycling systems, efforts at conservation, and repairs of leaky municipal water pipes will all need to be considered as possible solutions.

Fighting crime, together with devising creative ways to deal with an ever-increasing prison population, will continue to present new and important challenges. Shaka Senghor spent nineteen years in prison for murder. Since his release in 2010, he's become a teacher at the University of Michigan, a published author, a speaker, and an MIT Media Lab Director's Fellow. His current focus is on #Cut50, an initiative aimed at reducing the U.S. prison population by half. He believes that prison reform can help to address our nation's need for labor and reduce recidivism. What do you think?

Immigration, which already affects millions of families, border security, and the needs of a changing U.S. labor market also need to be addressed. In 1970, there were fewer than one million people in the United States from Mexico, Honduras, Guatemala, Nicaragua, and El Salvador. Today, America is home to more than fourteen million undocumented immigrants from these countries. In recent years, drug cartel-related violence has increased in many northern Mexican cities, causing a further increase in illegal drugs and undocumented immigrants coming across the border undetected. Reforms in U.S. legislation will be required to address this social, economic, and political reality. How might you be able to help?

Gun ownership will continue to be a hotly contested issue. Finding the right solution will require a balancing of Second Amendment concerns and practical realities. The Second Amendment to the U.S. Constitution guarantees individuals the right to bear arms. This is an important and fundamental right. Some, including many of our founding fathers, believe that the "right to bear arms" is a right upon which all other rights may someday depend. Yet, gun-related deaths and injuries are reaching unprecedented levels—levels not found in any other civilized country. According to the Children's Defense Fund, between 1979 and 1997, gunfire killed nearly eighty thousand children and teens in America—twenty-five thousand more than the total number of American soldiers killed in Vietnam. Firearms wounded an additional 320,000 children during this same period. The American Bar Association reports that American children are twelve times more likely to die from gun injuries than are youth in all other industrialized nations combined. The Centers for Disease Control tells us that the risk of suicide for 15- through 19-year-olds is five times greater for those living in a home with guns. These issues need to be examined and addressed in a way that advances our common social interests. Both sides of this debate have deeply held beliefs for good reasons. Arguments offered on both sides, when thoughtfully and objectively considered, have merit. In order to arrive at the best solution, all logical positions must be given thoughtful consideration. Resolving these issues will require significant thought, study, debate, and compromise. Think about how you might be able to play a role in impacting the issues that you care about and how you can bring about the changes you want to see.

Be Prepared to Change Direction and Adapt

Over forty years ago, Intel cofounder Gordon Moore observed, in what later became known as "Moore's Law," that the transistor count of computer processors doubles every eighteen months. With each doubling, comes a huge leap in computing power. In the years since Moore made that observation, the transistor count of computer processors has climbed from approximately two thousand to more than four billion. One consequence of this, which we can all relate to, is that our iPhone 6 now has more computing power than the computers NASA used to land a man on the moon.

It's difficult, if not impossible, to imagine the potential consequences of computer power doubling every two years. At that rate, the power of computers will increase by a factor of one million over the next forty years. Computer visionary Bill Joy pointed out that jet travel is faster than walking by a factor of one hundred, and we have all seen how that has changed the world. Nothing in our experience prepares us for what the world will be like forty years from now. This raises a multitude of issues including, but not limited to, the potential for radical shifts in employment and income inequality.

In *The Second Machine Age*, Erik Brynjolfsson and Andrew McAfee, of the Massachusetts Institute of Technology (MIT), asked what jobs will be left once computing power enables inexpensive, computerized solutions to problems that previously required costly human engagement.

Economist John Maynard Keynes made the prediction, decades ago, that society is heading toward a period of technological unemployment. Keynes predicted that society would discover ways to increase labor efficiency more rapidly than it would find new uses for labor.

Industries and workers that may soon be transformed and/or replaced by computers, include the following:

+ Transportation

+ Logistics

+ Construction and production

+ Bookkeepers

+ Travel agents

+ Legal aides

+ Cashiers

+ Telemarketers

+ Call center operators

+ Office workers and administrative support staff

In *The Future of Employment: How Susceptible Are Jobs to Computerisation?*, Carl Benedikt Frey, Oxford Martin School, University of Oxford, and Michael A. Osborne, Department of Engineering Science, University of Oxford, United Kingdom, estimate that 47 percent of total U.S. employment is in the high-risk category of potentially becoming automated over the next several decades.

As industrial robots become more advanced with enhanced senses and dexterity, they will be able to perform a wider array of nonroutine manual tasks. Google has already introduced a driverless car. In 2016, Ford will begin testing self-driving Fusion Hybrids on the roads in

California. In May of 2015, Daimler began testing the first self-driving semitruck on the highways of Nevada.

The number-one job held by American men (2.9 million of them) is truck driver. The number-one job held by American women (three million of them) is administrative assistant. Both of these occupations and many more are likely to be performed by computers rather than humans in the near future.

A video of the Tesla manufacturing plant on YouTube shows how a Tesla Model S goes from raw materials to a finished automobile, with the help of 160 robotic machines. What is most amazing about the video is how few human workers are required to create a Tesla Model S.

A company called Momentum Machines, in San Francisco, has designed a fully automated burger assembly line that replaces burger line cooks entirely. It cooks the meat, slices and dices all of the fresh ingredients, and fully assembles the finished product. Moreover, it does it faster, more consistently, and more economically than human workers. By replacing human workers, the machine reduces labor costs, liability, management duties, and space requirements. A significant percentage of the current 3.6 million fast food workers will be impacted by the use of machines designed to do their jobs, faster, more efficiently, and more cost effectively.

In May 2015, McDonald's employees protested outside McDonald's corporate headquarters in Chicago, demanding higher wages. At the same time, we are seeing mounting pressures to increase workers' wages, we are seeing innovations in technology that provide business owners with viable options to reduce labor costs and improve business performance by eliminating jobs performed by costly human workers. The greater the pressure to increase minimum wages, the more pressure employers may feel to replace low-skilled workers with machines. At the same time that improvements in technology are eliminating jobs, society must confront the challenge of creating even more jobs, with livable wages, to satisfy the needs of our existing and growing population. How will society meet this challenge? This is something we all need to be thinking about.

Former U.S. Treasury Secretary Lawrence Summers says that these issues will be "the defining economic feature of our era."

However, machines are not good at everything. As Brynjolfsson notes,

> Machines are not very good at motivating, nurturing,
> caring and comforting people. Human interactions
> are important and, so far at least, machines are wholly
> inadequate for those kind[s] of tasks.

Some argue that automation need not lead to mass unemployment. Instead, they see these technologies as tools that will allow people to achieve more. People cooperating with machines, rather than competing against them (what Brynjolfsson refers to as "racing with machines"), can achieve more than either could achieve independently.

According to Alan Manning, professor of economics at the London School of Economics:

> History teaches us that labor markets are able to recover
> from the changes brought upon them by technological
> change.

Manning argues,

> There will be people who have spent 20 or 30 years
> specialized in a job who will suddenly find that there
> is no demand for their skills any longer. They suffer
> big losses but in the long run … no young people go
> into those jobs, they go into something else and there
> is always something else to go into.

But Brynjolfsson says society shouldn't expect that people will simply adapt to the employment opportunities afforded to them by new technologies. To adjust to the labor upheaval that followed the industrial revolution, a long-term overhaul of our educational systems was essential, which is an approach that may need to be repeated. Brynjolfsson adds:

> If you look back to the first machine age, the vast majority
> of Americans worked in agriculture. Now it's less than
> two percent. Those people [working in agriculture]
> didn't simply become unemployed, they reskilled.

> One of the best ideas that America had was mass
> primary education. That's one of the reasons it became

an economic leader. We put a lot of effort into reskilling people in these earlier eras. It was very costly and not simple, but ultimately it was successful.

Brynjolfsson emphasizes that the commitment to education needs to continue. He also argues that lifelong learning will be essential for people to keep pace with the changing demands of roles constantly being reshaped by technology: "We have to reinvent education and reskilling … people are going to have to take it upon themselves to more aggressively learn these skills … it's going to be a case of lifelong learning and continuously reskilling."

To remain valuable, in this latest machine age, Brynjolfsson and McAfee argue that people will need to focus on learning skills that are tricky for computers, such as ideation (the creation of new ideas), large-frame pattern recognition, and complex communication.

Although the science, technology, engineering, and mathematics (STEM) fields provide some of the most rewarding careers in America today, that may not be true tomorrow. As technology advances, the most valuable human skills, those that society and the economy may increasingly value more than any others, may be our deeply human interpersonal abilities: empathy, sensitivity, collaboration, story-telling, relationship building and leading.

According to the research firm Oxford Economics, employers' top priorities already include relationship building, cultural sensitivity, brainstorming, co-creativity, and the ability to manage diverse employees— essentially, the right-brained skills of social interaction.

Meg Bear, Oracle group vice president, says, "Empathy is the critical 21st Century skill."

As technology advances, the demand for these skills is only going to increase. Those who can build relationships, collaborate, and lead— those who can engage clients with humor, energy, sensitivity, and generosity—will be tomorrow's most sought after employees.

Summers may well be correct in referring to this as the "the defining economic feature of our era." We need to be thinking about how humans will continue to add value in a world where computing power and the opportunities made possible by that computing power double every eighteen months. We need to think about how humans will "race with machines" and understand that it will require us to remain flexible, adaptable, and multidimensional. Above all, it will require that we maintain and develop all of the qualities that make us uniquely human.

Be Thoughtful about Your Choices

Life is not "one size fits all." What might be the right choice for one individual may be the wrong choice for another. One thing is clear: Life is all about choice. The choices we make are the most important factors in determining the lives that we lead. As you design and lead your life, you will need to make conscious choices every day. Some of these choices, even choices that appear insignificant at the time, may later prove to be significant or even life changing. You, therefore, need to think very carefully about every choice you make. This is even more critical with regard to choices that may be permanent or have long-term consequences.

Make choices that are right for you. Understand that each choice you make will have consequences. Perhaps most significantly, try to anticipate the full range of consequences that may flow from your choices, and accept the truth that you alone are responsible for the consequences of your choices.

Your Opportunities Are Virtually Unlimited

Albert Einstein said, "Imagination is more important than knowledge." The opportunities available to you are virtually limitless and truly extraordinary. You are limited only by your imagination, courage, and commitment. Life is short. As anyone over 40 will tell you, the years pass very quickly. You only have one life, and you alone have the power to design it. If possible, try to discover something you love, and try to do it well. Try to do something that inspires your dedication and commitment. Try to do something that maximizes your innate gifts and brings you happiness. Try to do something that is meaningful to you.

In Hinduism, your calling or the thing you were meant to do that is closest to your essential nature, is called your dharma. In Buddhism, dharma is ideal truth. Much more than finding work you love, it means finding work that will be supported by your innate gifts. It means the "right way of living" or the "path of righteousness." It means adopting behaviors that are in accordance with the order that makes life and the universe possible.

If you are truly passionate about your work, it will never seem like work. You will wake up every morning excited to meet the challenges and opportunities your work presents. When you do something you love, it doesn't feel like work. It becomes something you actually crave.

Most people work for a living. Some take any job that will pay the bills and believe they have no other choice. For some people, that may be true. They may have limited choices. But if you're reading this book, that's probably not true for you. Individuals who have the capacity and desire to read a book on self-improvement have the potential to find work that they love, work that they are passionate about, work that allows them to lead happy, successful, and meaningful lives. You have many choices. Be thoughtful while you discover your own essential nature, your own truth. Choose wisely.

CHAPTER FOUR

Developing Your Plan of Action

ACCORDING TO THE U.S. Bureau of Labor, there were 3.4 million unemployed youth (ages 16–24) in July of 2014. This represents a youth unemployment rate of 14.3 percent. Worldwide, more than 75 million young people are without a job.

You are certainly not entitled to one of the limited jobs available; however, if you are focused and determined, you absolutely can get a job if you want one. You can do much more if you're motivated. You simply need to make the required effort.

You may be thinking, "I don't need a job." Or, "I'm going to be a star on YouTube." Great! I hope so. If you're creative and determined, you may be the next YouTube sensation. You may be coding the next dotcom phenomenon, even better. But until you reach some level of success that allows you to generate income, you may need a job to pay the bills. Keep that in mind as you plan your next moves. Don't do anything to limit your options. On the contrary, always be thinking about how you can increase your options.

Explore Your Options: Discover What Career Best Suits You

Some people are fortunate and focused. Their life's goals appear very early and very clearly. Some take longer to acquire a clear vision of their future.

David Ogilvy, who wrote *Ogilvy on Advertising*, had a privileged upbringing. He went to a private Scottish school called Fettes, but he was too preoccupied to do any work and was expelled. For the next seventeen years, while his friends were establishing themselves as doctors, lawyers, civil servants, and politicians, he adventured throughout the world, uncertain of his life's purpose. He worked as a chef in Paris, a door-to-door salesman of cooking stoves in England, a social worker in the Edinburgh slums, and an associate of George Gallup doing research for the motion picture industry. Ogilvy had expected to become prime minister of England when he grew up. Instead, he became an advertising agent on Madison Avenue and eventually built one of the world's most profitable and successful agencies. His book contains invaluable insights and is a must-read for anyone interested in advertising or business.

Ogilvy was a fascinating man. Given his privileged status, he was expected to pursue a more traditional career in politics, law, medicine, or banking. Yet he knew that these professions didn't fit his personality. In rejecting these traditional callings, he was a rebel and a nonconformist, but his nonconformity was measured. It was that measured nonconformity that allowed him to bridge the creative world and the corporate world.

He was a creative genius who didn't immediately understand or identify his calling or purpose in life. After being expelled from Fettes, it took him nearly two decades to find his life's purpose. Ogilvy later became one of the all-time greatest figures in advertising. In fact, he was called the "Father of Advertising."

Others are far more focused. They may know what they want to do at an early age. However, as Ogilvy's example illustrates, a person's early identification of purpose is not necessary for success. A curiosity about life, creativity, determination, and a commitment to excel are far more important.

Prepare for Success

Legendary basketball coach Bobby Knight said, "Everyone has the will to win. It's those who prepare to win that do." Countless articles have been written about YouTube and other web-based businesses. If this interests you, go online and read everything you can about the opportunities that exist in this area. Learn how to create content. Learn how to monetize your work. See what others are doing. Learn how to use social media to make your content go viral. *The Anatomy of Buzz* by Emanuel Rosen and *Guerrilla Marketing* by Jay Conrad Levinson are great books filled with useful tips on how to generate buzz for your content. All of this can be researched online. When I began to write this book, I knew absolutely nothing about publishing or marketing a book. I learned nearly everything I needed online.

Khan Academy (www.khanacademy.org) is a nonprofit online resource with the mission of providing a free, world-class education for anyone, anywhere. Bill Gates' kids use it. Khan offers courses that cover all levels of math and science, economics and finance, arts and humanities, computer programing, and even test preparation for admission to colleges and graduate programs. It is truly an incredible online educational resource. And it's free!

Even if you didn't do well enough in high school to get into college, you can learn everything you need to know at Khan Academy. You can learn whatever you need to know about how to use a computer or even program one. Kahn Academy can help you prepare for and take your college entrance exams. For some students, Khan's tutoring is all they need to succeed in high school or college. This online school has given others a second chance to overcome the mistakes they made in high school or college. We don't always get second chances in life, yet here is one that could move your life in a whole new direction.

You are literally surrounded by a wealth of free information. Take advantage of it. If you don't have a computer, use one at your public library. If you don't know how to use a computer, ask for help. There are organizations in nearly every community whose mission is to help people gain access to information and assistance. Team up with that nerdy kid in your neighborhood who has a computer and knows how to use it. Leverage your relationships. Find synergies between your talents and those of others. Offer to partner with others and combine your talents, skills, and resources.

I remember one of my law professors telling me, "Never forget the three P's: preparation, preparation, preparation." I never did forget. During my thirty years of practicing law, I always tried to be more prepared than anyone I was dealing with. When I argued before the U.S. Supreme Court, I felt as if I knew more about the subject of my argument than anyone—except the nine justices I was appearing before. I won 9/0. Preparation is key. The nature and amount of preparation required depends on what it is that you are trying to accomplish.

For an athlete, preparation might include mapping out a training regime, establishing a diet, creating a practice schedule, studying various techniques and strategies, or watching films of opposing players or teams. If you really want to be a professional athlete, be prepared for tremendous sacrifices. Michael Jordan was known for extending his own practices well beyond that of his team's already grueling practice schedule. He is not alone. Tiger Woods has hit millions of golf balls and spent thousands of hours just practicing his putting. All of the greatest athletes train relentlessly!

For an aspiring entertainer, preparation might include writing songs, practicing an instrument, voice training, dance rehearsal, acting classes, live performances, or recording sessions. The sacrifice, dedication, and effort required of a successful entertainer is equal to that of a professional athlete.

For starting a new business, the preparation required might involve creating a formal written business plan, creating a prototype, identifying sources of capital, finding a location, hiring staff, researching product sources or producing a product, attracting customers, and making sales. The life of a successful entrepreneur is no less demanding than that of a professional athlete or entertainer.

Peter Guber, chairman and CEO of Mandalay Entertainment, described the life of an entrepreneur as follows:

> You're floating down the Amazon in a blinding rainstorm, there's a waterfall ahead and Indians are shooting arrows at you from the banks, as you look back, the guys who are supposed to be paddling, are drilling holes in the bottom of the boat.

Whatever it is that you want in life—be prepared. Begin by being prepared to work hard.

Seek Out Opportunities to Learn from the Best

Ogilvy had worked as a chef at the Hotel Majestic in Paris with famous head chef Monsieur Pitard. In describing how he planned to run his advertising agency, Ogilvy points to Pitard as his inspiration. One thing that distinguishes incredibly successful men and women is that they have had the good fortune to be inspired by another's greatness and have carried forward that standard of excellence in their own work.

If you are fortunate enough to find yourself in the presence of greatness or have the opportunity to know or work with an individual whose example you would like to emulate, I hope you will recognize the importance of that opportunity and capitalize on it by learning and internalizing all that you can.

If you want a mentor, understand that mentors are attracted to people who have talent and show promise. So exhibit talent. Show promise. Once you identify someone you would like as a mentor, figure out how to help that person. Never ask or expect them to help you. If they eventually do help you on anything, it means they see something in you that they like. They may see your promise and potential. They may see how you could be able to help them in some way.

Show gratitude. Thank them for their time, support, and interest. Work tirelessly to impress them. Earn their support and admiration; deserve it but don't expect it. If it comes, cherish it. One good friend is worth a thousand acquaintances. If a prospective mentor doesn't respond to you, it may mean that you haven't done enough to impress him or he needs more time to see if you stay the course. It may mean that the person sees something or had heard something he doesn't like about you. More likely, it may simply mean that the person is too busy or not inclined toward mentorship. Whatever the reason, don't blame the individual you admire for not noticing you, acknowledging you, or embracing you. Don't assume you deserve it. You may not. You're certainly not entitled to a mentor. Mentors are a rare gift occasionally bestowed upon a select few. If you are fortunate enough to attract one, treasure that person and the incredible opportunity that his or her guidance represents.

Winston Churchill drank like a fish. He was rude to fools. He was said to be extravagant, capricious, and inconsiderate to his staff. Yet it would be difficult to imagine a greater honor than working with such a man. Churchill's Chief of Staff, Lord Alanbrooke, wrote,

> I shall always look back on the years I worked with him as some of the most difficult and trying ones in my life. For all that, I thank God that I was given the opportunity of working alongside of such a man, and of having my eyes opened to the fact that occasionally such supermen exist on this earth.

Great people all seem to have one thing in common—a reverence for excellence. If you share that reverence and exhibit excellence, you are more likely to attract them. You may even become one yourself.

Create a Detailed Plan of Action

Once Ogilvy determined his purpose, he developed a clear plan of action. He began by deciding that his pursuit of perfection would need to be uncompromising. Ogilvy had a multifaceted plan of action for launching his agency. He began by inviting journalists from the advertising trade press to lunch. He told them of his plan to build a great agency, and they helped him. He was bright, well-mannered, charming, and articulate. He made a great impression. They quoted him frequently. They printed every press release he sent them.

He spoke at advertising industry functions on topics that were sure to generate discussion and attention, bringing added attention to himself and his agency. He made friends with people whose jobs brought them into contact with major advertisers, researchers, public relations consultants, management engineers, and advertising space salesmen. He sent regular progress reports to six hundred key figures representing every walk of life.

In sum, he aggressively promoted himself, and he did so brilliantly and tactfully. The same plan could be applied to a wide variety of businesses. It would be equally successful today.

Virtually every successful endeavor begins with a plan. Once you identify what you want to do, you need to plan how to achieve your objectives. Many young people claim that they intend to be successful. Yet very few understand the level of sacrifice and commitment required to achieve that success. Even fewer are willing to make the sacrifices required to achieve their goals. The reality is that few of these young people will ever fully achieve their objectives. Why? They won't make the commitment or devote the time and effort required to achieve their objectives. Those who truly want to be successful plan, prepare, and sacrifice. They are more successful than their competition because they work much harder.

A plan of action is simply a checklist that identifies the things that you need to do to move from where you are to where you want to be. Develop your plan of action by making a list of the items you believe would be helpful in making your dream a reality. Then prioritize and begin working on each item on that list. Remember the three P's, but also be creative, be resourceful, be driven, be hopeful, be courageous, and be committed.

Life can be exciting and exceptional, but success requires hard work. To be successful, it is not enough that you really want to be successful,. In order to reach your goals, you have to *make the effort required* to reach your goals—whatever they may be.

Kevin O'Leary, founder of O'Leary Financial Group and Shark on ABC's Shark Tank, says, "'To be or not to be?' is not the question. The question is: What are you willing to do in order to be what you want to be?"

The more you want it, the more you will work to achieve it, and the harder you work, the more likely you are to achieve it.

Action is magic. Determine your destination. Develop your plan and take action.

Chapter Five

Making the Right Choices

EVERYONE HAS THE POWER of choice. Regardless of what position you are in now, what conditions you were raised under, or what may have happened to you, you have the power to choose how to respond and to choose what you will do next.

Dealing with life's challenges can be extremely difficult. But how you decide to deal with what you encounter will always be a matter of choice. Never lose sight of that fact. You will always have the power of choice, even if it is limited to choosing how to react to events or circumstances that you did not choose.

A great deal happens in life that is beyond our control. There are many things that we do not choose. We don't choose our parents. We don't choose many of the experiences, disabilities, or tragedies that may be thrust upon us, but we do have the power to choose how we respond to them.

Choices Have Consequences

We all make choices every day. These choices can profoundly affect the lives we lead. Good choices generally have positive consequences. Bad choices generally have negative consequences. The consequences of some choices may be immediate, intended, and obvious. Other consequences may be less immediate, less obvious and unintended. To make an informed decision, you need to anticipate and consider all of the potential consequences of your choices. You need to think ahead.

Ingesting certain drugs may cause you to feel better or enhance a social experience. This consequence is immediate and anticipated, but there may be unanticipated consequences. Each of us has a unique physiology. We all have different physical traits, unique medical conditions, and a wide range of tolerances. How your friend's body reacts to a chemical substance may be very different from how your body reacts to the very same chemical substance. What your friend found to be a wonderful experience could turn out to be a very negative or even a deadly experience for you. What you found to be a great experience on one occasion could prove to be a very negative experience on the next occasion.

Taking certain drugs may also cause you to fail a drug test and result in your being unable to obtain or retain your desired employment. It may lead to addiction and lessen your ability to choose going forward. It may temporarily impair your senses or motor skills and lead to an accident resulting in arrest, injury, or death. You may know of someone who died from a drug overdose. Do you believe that person wanted to die? If it wasn't a suicide, it was a miscalculation. It was a failure to anticipate unforeseen consequences. These are just some of the unanticipated consequences that could flow from a simple decision to put a pill in your mouth.

Choosing to accept a ride from a stranger, walking down a dark alley, venturing into a bad or unfamiliar neighborhood, dropping out of school, or hanging out with the wrong crowd can all be life-changing choices.

Steven Smith was an All Pac-10 Conference point guard for Arizona State University from 1991 through 1994. In 1994, he made the decision to become involved in the Arizona State point shaving scandal. Smith allegedly received $20,000 for shaving points in the game against Oregon State on January 28, 1994. He was arrested and pleaded guilty to conspiracy charges. Smith was sentenced to one year and one day in prison, but that was not the true cost of Smith's poor decision.

Prior to this incident, Smith was widely regarded as a top college player. He would have been an early NBA draft pick. Instead, because of the scandal that surrounded him, no team would draft him. His poor decision cost him and his family much more than one year in prison. It cost them his NBA career. It changed his entire family's life forever. You need to learn from his mistake and from the mistakes of others. If not, you will learn the hard way from your own mistakes. Be smart—learn from the mistakes of others and avoid making your own.

Think Ahead

The list of possible poor choices is virtually endless. You need to learn how to make good choices regardless of the circumstances. You need to learn to think ahead. A grand master of chess will anticipate his opponent's moves as many as fourteen moves out. He will consider each of his possible moves, each of his opponent's possible responses, and each of his possible follow-up responses. He will play out a significant portion of the game in his head before he makes his first move. Life is no different. To make the right choices, you must anticipate and consider the possible consequences of your actions. You may not be able to anticipate all potential consequences, but you can usually anticipate many. The more you can think ahead and consider what could happen, the better off you'll be. Make the effort. Think about the potential consequences of your actions—before you act.

One way to determine if you are making a good decision is to ask people whose opinions you value what they think. Getting meaningful input can often help us make better choices. Multiple opinions from people with different perspectives can be especially helpful. If several people who normally have different perspectives are all telling you the same thing, you may want to think very carefully before disregarding that advice. Always remember that you have the power of choice. Think ahead, choose wisely, and accept responsibility for your choices.

CHAPTER SIX

The Meaning and Importance of Character

CHARACTER IS THE SUM of the stable and distinctive qualities built into an individual's life that determine his or her choices regardless of circumstances. Character consists of the unique qualities that define each one of us. It guides our responses to any situation or circumstance. It determines why we do the things we do and how we do them. Good character is perhaps the single most essential quality necessary for success. Without it, no one will want to hire you or do business with you. In fact, a flawed or weak character will eventually cause others to avoid having anything to do with you.

Dr. Martin Luther King said, "I have a dream that my four little children will one day live in a nation where they will not be judged by the color of their skin but by the content of their character." Dr. King understood and embraced the importance of character because he had great character. It was his strength of character that allowed him to inspire a nation.

Dominic Randolph is the headmaster at Riverdale Country School. Riverdale is one of New York City's most prestigious private schools, with a 104-year-old campus in the wealthiest part of the Bronx. Tuition starts at $38,500 per year, and that's for prekindergarten. David Levin is the co-founder of the KIPP network of charter schools in New York City. KIPP operates a nonprofit network of eleven free, open-enrollment public charter schools in the Bronx, Brooklyn, Harlem, and Washington Heights. Randolph and Levin manage very different schools with very different student populations. Yet both men have a common vision of what is missing from our current public and private educational systems. They both believe that the most critical missing piece in education is character development.

In a September 14, 2011, article, entitled, "What if the Secret to Success Is Failure," by Paul Tough, Randolph says,

> Whether it's the pioneer in the Conestoga wagon or someone coming here in the 1920s from southern Italy, there was this idea in America that if you worked hard and you showed real grit, that you could be successful. Strangely, we've now forgotten that. People who have an easy time of things, who get 800s on their SAT's, I worry that those people get feedback that everything they're doing is great. And I think as a result, we are actually setting them up for long-term failure. When that person suddenly has to face up to a difficult moment, then I think they're screwed, to be honest. I don't think they've grown the capacities to be able to handle that.

Levin works with a less affluent and more ethnically diverse student population. But he shares Randolph's concern. As Levin watched the progress of KIPP alumni, he noticed that the students who succeeded in college were not necessarily the ones who had excelled academically at KIPP; they were the ones with exceptional character strengths, like optimism, persistence, and social intelligence. These were the students who were able to recover from a bad grade and resolve to do better next time. They were able to bounce back from a fight with their parents or their boyfriend. They had the willpower to resist the urge to go out to campus parties and instead stayed home and studied. He came to see these traits as an indispensable part of making it to graduation day.

Randolph and Levin both met with Martin Seligman, a psychology professor at the University of Pennsylvania, and Christopher Peterson, a psychology professor at the University of Michigan, to discuss the impact of character on students and learning. Seligman and Peterson had just coauthored an eight hundred-page treatise on character entitled, *Character Strengths and Virtues: A Handbook and Classification.*

What Seligman and Peterson found through their extensive research is that cultivating essential character strengths represented a reliable path to "the good life," a life that was not just happy but also meaningful and fulfilling.

Angela Duckworth is an assistant professor in Seligman's department. When she applied to the doctoral program at Penn, she stated,

> The problem, I think, is not only the schools but also the students themselves ... here's why: learning is hard. True, learning is fun, exhilarating and gratifying—but it is also often daunting, exhausting, and sometimes discouraging ... . To help chronically low-performing but intelligent students, educators and parents must first recognize that character is at least as important as intellect.

Duckworth's early research showed that measures of self-control can be a more reliable predictor of students' grade-point averages than their IQs. But while self-control seemed to be a critical ingredient in attaining basic success, Duckworth came to feel it wasn't as relevant for outstanding achievement. People who accomplished great things, she noticed, often combined a passion for a single mission with an unswerving dedication to achieve that mission—no matter what the obstacles were and how long it might take. She decided she needed to name this quality, and she chose the word "grit."

Levin and Randolph asked Duckworth to use the new methods and tools she was developing to help them investigate the question of how to instill character values at KIPP and Riverdale. They asked Peterson if he could identify a set of strengths that were, according to his research, especially likely to predict life satisfaction and high achievement. They settled on a final list: zest, grit, self-control, social intelligence, gratitude, optimism, and curiosity.

In 2008, a national organization called the Character Education Partnership published a paper that divided character education into two categories: programs that develop "moral character," embodying ethical values like fairness, generosity, and integrity; and those that address "performance character," including values like effort, diligence, and perseverance.

Character Traits That Lead to a Happy and Successful Life

Character includes multiple character traits. Some traits that I believe can lead to a happy, successful, and meaningful life include honesty, integrity, honor, truthfulness, dependability, diligence, humility, punctuality, sincerity, tolerance, and generosity. Throughout this book, I sometimes refer to these positive character traits as "core values."

Honesty is broader than truthfulness. It extends beyond what you say and includes all of your actions and dealings with others. It's being fair, just, forthright, and truthful. At all times, in all circumstances, be honest.

Integrity means being true to your word. It means honoring your commitments, being dependable and trustworthy. A person who has integrity is a person you can count on. Have integrity and surround yourself only with people who have integrity.

Honor means taking personal responsibility to uphold what is pure, right, true, and just. A person with honor always does the right thing regardless of consequences. A person of honor is a beautiful and enlightened individual. Of all the great values, honor is perhaps the most important and rare. If you have honor, you are, simply by virtue of that quality, already successful. Be honorable.

Truthfulness means never lying or withholding information. Even a small lie can ruin an individual's career, destroy a marriage, or end a lifelong friendship. Be truthful in all your dealings, and accept nothing less from those with whom you associate.

Dependability means doing what you agreed to do, even if it means making unexpected sacrifices. It means showing up for work on time, doing your job well, meeting your deadlines, and supporting others. It is a cornerstone of success. You cannot be successful without it. Be dependable.

Diligence means perseverance, hard work, and constant effort to accomplish a given task. It means using your best efforts to overcome obstacles and achieve your objectives. It means doing whatever is required to meet your goals. Success requires diligence. Be diligent.

Humility means being modest and selfless. It means giving credit where credit is due. It is the opposite of being boastful. It includes being willing to undertake unglamorous tasks and graciously accepting the sacrifices involved. Having humility is a sign of strength. Be humble.

Punctuality means showing respect and esteem for others by showing up on time and meeting deadlines. Not being punctual is extremely inconsiderate and disrespectful. Successful people pride themselves on being punctual and expect others to be punctual. Be punctual.

Sincerity is authenticity. It means being who you are. It means saying only what you believe and meaning what you say. Sincerity is extremely persuasive and compelling because it is real. It comes from the heart. Be sincere.

Tolerance means accepting others for who they are. It means being open to new ideas, people, cultures, and customs. It means being open to alternative points of view. It means understanding the value of diversity. Be tolerant.

Generosity means treating all people with respect even when they can't do anything for you. It means being gracious and kind to everyone you meet. It means recognizing that every human being, regardless of status, deserves respect, consideration, and happiness. It means helping and caring about others. Be generous.

Mistakes and Errors in Judgment

You may be thinking, "How can anyone live up to *all of these standards?*" The answer is—no one can. None of us can. Absolute perfection is neither expected nor required. To err is human. We all make mistakes. But we can try to do what is right, and it is by constantly trying that we build, over time, both our characters and our reputations.

David Petraeus served as director of the Central Intelligence Agency (CIA) from September 6, 2011, until his resignation on November 9, 2012. Prior to being appointed director of the CIA, Petraeus was a highly decorated four-star general, who had served over 37 years in the United States Army. He commanded U.S. Forces in Afghanistan and oversaw all coalition forces in Iraq. His entire life, except for one episode, evidenced a man of great character and integrity.

On November 9, 2012, General Petraeus resigned from his position as director of the CIA, citing his extramarital affair, which reportedly had been discovered in the course of an FBI investigation. In January

2015, officials reported that FBI and Justice Department prosecutors had recommended bringing felony charges against Petraeus for allegedly providing classified information to his mistress while serving as the CIA's director. Eventually, Petraeus pleaded guilty to one misdemeanor charge of mishandling classified information.

Throughout his forty-plus years of military and public service, Petraeus demonstrated incredible character. He gave this country a life of service, dedication, and leadership that enriched all of us immensely. His lapse in judgment, his decision to have an affair and share classified information was tragic, not in terms of what it did to the country, but in terms of what it did to diminish the reputation of this otherwise amazing man.

Some may disagree, but I still see David Petraeus as a hero and a man of great character. I look at the sum total of his life, including his moment of weakness, and I see a man whom I would trust, a man I would do business with, and a man I would be very proud to call my friend. I do not see a perfect man, but I know that no man or woman is perfect. I don't expect or require perfection of my friends or my business associates—if I did, I wouldn't have any friends, and I couldn't do any business. None of us are capable of perfection. Great character does not require that we are perfect and error free. We all make mistakes. I know I have made mistakes in my life, and I don't know a single soul who hasn't.

In my view, having great character does not require that you never make mistakes. If it did, no one could be said to have great character. Instead, it requires that you work hard to avoid mistakes and make good choices. Each person that you deal with will judge you based upon his or her own personal standards. Some may require less of you. Others may require more.

In the end, your character and your reputation will be assessed based on your words and your deeds. Your mistakes will be evaluated based upon their nature and your intent. Innocent and trivial mistakes may offer some insight into your character, but are unlikely to significantly impact your reputation unless they are ongoing. More significant mistakes or errors in judgment, especially those that are intentional, can say a great deal about your character and have a profoundly negative impact on your reputation. We all make mistakes—people with great character simply make fewer of them. Their mistakes are also normally unintentional and less significant.

Given that you are bound to make certain mistakes in your life, it is important that you know what do when that happens. Having great character requires that you admit your mistakes. It requires that you do whatever is required to correct your mistakes. It requires that you accept responsibility for your mistakes and graciously accept the consequences of your mistakes. To do otherwise only compounds your mistakes and evidences a serious lack of character. Part of accepting responsibility for our mistakes includes apologizing to those we have hurt or disrespected. Be honest and humble. Admit when your wrong, acknowledge your mistakes and always be willing to apologize.

Most people are, by nature, very forgiving. We want to forgive those who have trespassed against us even when we have been hurt and disappointed by their actions. We believe in second chances. But in doing so, we expect those who have made mistakes to admit their mistakes and to accept responsibility for their mistakes. Always remember this! I cannot overstate the importance of this message. Never allow your poor handling of your mistakes to say more about your character than the mistakes themselves. Instead, use your mistakes as opportunities to show the true substance of your character by immediately owning and accepting responsibility for your mistakes. These are critically important concepts.

Successful people understand and embrace these core values. Moreover, most of them expect that all of the people they work with and associate with, both personally and professionally, embrace these same core values. Regardless of your social or economic condition or circumstances, when you practice these core values, others will respect and admire you. You will build lasting and important personal and professional relationships. Conversely, failure to adopt and practice these core values will undermine and/or preclude such relationships and lead to failure and despair.

A person's reputation is his or her most valuable asset. It can take a lifetime to build and only a single poor choice to destroy. Build your reputation by practicing these core values. Then guard and protect your reputation zealously. Nothing you possess will ever be more important. "Regard your good name as the richest jewel you can possibly be possessed of" (Socrates, Greek philosopher).

Unintended Consequences of the Pressure to Succeed

Race to Nowhere, a 2009 documentary film about the stresses facing primarily privileged American high school students, has become an underground hit in many wealthy suburbs. The movie paints a grim portrait of contemporary adolescence, ending with the story of an overachieving teenage girl who commits suicide, apparently because of the ever-increasing pressure to succeed that she felt at school and at home.

Race to Nowhere has helped to bring together a growing movement of psychologists and educators who argue that the systems and methods now in place to raise and educate well-off kids in the United States are, in fact, devastating them. Madeline Levine, a psychologist in Marin County who is the author of a best-selling book, *The Price of Privilege: How Parental Pressure and Material Advantage Are Creating a Generation of Disconnected and Unhappy Kids*, is a central figure in the film. In her book, Levine cites studies and surveys to back up her contention that children of affluent parents now exhibit "unexpectedly high rates of emotional problems beginning in junior high school." Levine says this is a direct result of the child-raising practices that prevail in well-off American homes. Wealthy parents today, she argues, are more likely to be emotionally distant from their children and, at the same time, insist on high levels of achievement, creating a potentially toxic blend of influences that can create "intense feelings of shame and hopelessness" in affluent children.

This can be a problem for all parents. As parents, we want to provide for our children. We want to give them everything they need. We want to shield and protect them. And yet, as Paul Tough correctly observes, "We all know—on some level, at least—that what kids need more than anything is a little hardship: some challenge, some deprivation that they can overcome, even if just to prove to themselves that they can. As a parent, you struggle with these thorny questions every day, and if you make the right call even half the time, you're lucky."

In the end, we need to understand that character is critical to success. As parents, we need to find ways to instill these moral and performance values while being conscious of the emotional pressures that our insistence on high-level performance can create.

Chapter Seven

How to Communicate Effectively

ONE OF THE ESSENTIAL skills required to manage all forms of social relationships is the ability to communicate effectively. Over the years, I have attempted to share some of the lessons I have learned with my family and others. At times, this effort has been very successful. In other instances, I have been unable to reach members of my own family on certain important issues.

I pride myself on being a skilled communicator. I served as Nevada's Attorney General, ran the state's largest law firm, and successfully argued (9/0) before the U.S. Supreme Court. Yet, at times, I have seen what I considered inescapable logic fall on deaf ears. If a highly trained professional advocate sometimes has difficulty communicating, I can only imagine how difficult it must be for others who have little or no training to get their messages across. I hope this information will help you to become a more effective communicator in every part of your life.

Barriers to Effective Communication

Effective communication can be exceedingly challenging and complex. It may even be impossible at times. The inability to communicate effectively with a child can be extremely frustrating and difficult for any parent to accept. That is the nature of parenting. The joy of parenting comes from meeting and overcoming the myriad of challenges presented. The obligation of parenting requires that we use our best efforts to overcome those challenges.

The human brain is a complex mechanism, and human beings are complex creatures. For a variety of reasons, not all attempts at communication are successful. Barriers to communication can even be physiological. Jay N. Giedd, chair of the division of child and adolescent psychiatry at the University of California, San Diego, wrote an article entitled "The Amazing Teen Brain," which appeared in the June 2015 issue of *Scientific American*. In this article, he explains that teenagers are more likely than children or adults to engage in risky behavior. Part of this is due to a mismatched development between two major regions of the brain. Giedd explains that development of the limbic system, which drives emotions, intensifies as puberty begins (between ages 10 to 12), and the system matures over the next several years. The brain's prefrontal cortex controls impulsive actions. It does not approach full development until a decade later.

Essentially, this means that from ages 12 until 25, teens are emotionally propelled by the limbic system while the prefrontal cortex, which is required to manage and control their emotional impulses, is not fully developed. *That leaves a decade of imbalance between emotional and contemplative thinking.* At times, this mismatch in the brain's regional development can cause teenagers to make poor decisions.

An important video on the teenage brain is "The Neuroanatomical Transformation of the Teenage Brain" by Jill Bolte Taylor, delivered at TEDxYouth@Indianapolis on February 21, 2013. You can find it on YouTube.com.

Understanding the physiological limitations of the teenage brain is important for parents who are trying to understand and cope with their teenagers' impulsive actions and poor choices. Being aware of these physiological limitations is equally important for teens, as they try to understand their emotions and avoid making poor choices.

Additional physiological limitations can also impact communication. Under certain circumstances, when people of any age are under severe emotional distress, the region of the brain responsible for emotion releases the chemicals adrenaline and cortisol. These chemicals can impair cognitive performance and interfere with the brain's ability to process logical information. When someone is under severe stress, the release of these chemicals can actually prevent the logical part of the brain from functioning properly. Therefore, if children are angry, depressed, or emotionally erratic, their ability to process logical information may actually be physiologically impaired. If we can learn to wait for these emotions caused by stress to subside, we can facilitate more effective communication.

Parents need to be alert to this issue. If your child is upset or highly emotional, that is one of the worst times to try and talk to them. Getting angry yourself, makes effective communication even less likely. In order to increase the likelihood of effective communication, you need emotional empathy. You need to recognize and address the emotional needs of others as well as your own. When you are trying to reach someone with a logical argument, understand that you are least likely to do so when either or both of you are upset.

We also need to be alert to the possibility of mental illness. One out of three people suffer from some form of mental illness. Severe and prolonged difficulties in communication can be a sign of mental illness. The social stigma often associated with mental illness can sometimes cause parents to fail to recognize or accept the fact that their child may be suffering from a mental illness. Parents want the best for their children. As a result, they can be slow to acknowledge or accept the fact that their child may have serious mental or emotional problems or limitations. They may even ignore warnings from teachers and counselors out of fear that their child may be held back or fail to progress in school. This is a mistake. In some cases, it is a mistake that can have tragic consequences.

Nancy Lanza was the first to be killed by her son, Adam Lanza, before he proceeded to slaughter twenty children and six adults on December 14, 2012, at Sandy Hook Elementary School in Newtown, Connecticut. Many family members of his victims blamed his mother for ignoring early signs of his mental illness. A report released by the Connecticut Office of the Child Advocate profiled the developmental and educational history of Adam Lanza. The report noted, "missed opportunities" by Lanza's mother, the school district, and multiple health care providers. It identified "warning signs and red flags" that should have alerted his mother, his teachers, and health care providers to his mental illness.

If you are having serious difficulty communicating with your children and if the information contained in this book does not help you to communicate with them more effectively, then seek professional help. Meet with school counselors. Ask them to refer you to community agencies that may be able to provide you with help and guidance. Get your children the counseling and professional assistance they need. As a parent, you have a responsibility to provide your children with the medical care that they require. Sickness can be mental and/or physical. Both require treatment. Ignoring, rationalizing, or failing to acknowledge serious mental health problems and early warning signs does a disservice to your child and may place your entire family and the community at risk.

We all need to understand the importance and the challenges of communication. We all need to be more verbal and to substitute verbal communication for aggressive physical approaches. We all need to learn how to express ourselves and communicate our thoughts, feelings, and ideas more clearly. We all need to learn how to actively listen and observe.

We all communicate verbally and nonverbally. However, not all of us communicate effectively. People who communicate effectively find that their communication skills often lead to success. Those who do not communicate effectively find that their poor communication skills can lead to misunderstandings and failure. Effective communication is about more than just exchanging information. It's also about understanding the emotions behind the information.

The Skills Required for Effective Communication

Effective communication utilizes a set of skills that include nonverbal communication, active listening, the ability to control your own stress, and the capacity to recognize and understand your emotions and those of the person you're communicating with. Listening is one of the most critical components of effective communication.

Understanding Nonverbal Communication

In his best-selling book, *What They Don't Teach You at Harvard Business School*, Mark H. McCormack discusses the importance of reading people. He explains how listening aggressively, observing aggressively, reading people's behavior, and using your insights can reveal critical information.

For anyone interested in business, his book is excellent. Developing the ability to understand and use nonverbal communication can help you understand and connect with others, express what you really mean, and build better, stronger relationships.

Active Listening

How do you become an effective listener? Focus on the speaker. What are the body language and other nonverbal cues saying? If you're not paying attention because you're reading emails or checking text messages, you're not listening effectively. Stay focused. Avoid interrupting. Avoid being judgmental. You don't have to agree with the speaker, but you do need to listen carefully to what he or she is saying. Listening carefully doesn't indicate agreement. It indicates understanding. The speaker needs to see that you understand what he is saying. Otherwise, the speaker will keep trying to make you understand. Demonstrating that you understand the other person's message allows her to stop talking and to listen to your message. This is an essential element of effective communication. If you are not a good listener, you simply cannot be an effective communicator. Many people are incapable of listening to what you are saying unless and until they believe that you understand their position. So listen to their position, and let them know that you truly do understand their position. Then tell them your position.

Richard Branson, founder of Virgin Group, says, "The most successful entrepreneurs I know all have excellent listening skills in common." John Marshall, who served as chief justice of the U.S. Supreme Court from 1801 to 1835, once said, "To listen well is as powerful a means of communication and influence as to talk well." Successful listening means not just understanding the information being communicated, but also understanding how the speaker feels about what he or she is saying.

While listening, show that you are genuinely interested in what's being said. Smile occasionally. Look at the person who's talking to you. Make sure your posture is open and inviting. Stay focused on what the other person is saying. The way you look, sit, listen, and react to another person reveals as much, if not more, about how you're feeling as your words do. Active listening also involves making sure you truly understand the speaker by occasionally repeating back, in your own words, what you think the person is communicating. You can say something like, "I want to be sure I understand what you're saying. Are you saying that you feel no one cares about your point of view?" The speaker will then let you know whether or not that is what she is trying to communicate. If she believes you have heard her, she will be more open to listening to your position. Active listening shows respect for the other person. It establishes that you are a reasonable person who is entitled to respect in return. It shows that you are committed to a full, fair, and rational dialogue. It makes you someone that others will want to communicate with. It makes you a far more effective communicator.

Communicating in Stressful Situations

Stress can also block communication. When stress becomes overwhelming, it can hamper effective communication by reducing your ability to think clearly and act appropriately. By learning to control your stress, you can face any emotions you're experiencing, regulate your feelings, and behave appropriately. If you feel stressed, take a moment to calm down before deciding to continue a conversation or postpone it. Take a few deep breaths. Try to think of something that is pleasant and relaxing. Normally, the best option may be to simply take a break. Go for a walk outside, if possible. Finding a quiet place to regain your composure can sometimes reduce stress in a matter of minutes. Don't just be open to compromise. Actively think about compromise positions that might satisfy the interests of all concerned.

Understanding How Emotions Influence Communication

Emotions also influence how we communicate. We need to understand our emotions and the emotions of those we are communicating with. If you are not in touch with your feelings, you'll have a hard time communicating your feelings and needs to others. Our ability to communicate effectively depends on our being connected to our feelings and those of others. Think about your feelings before communicating. Focus on what you are feeling and why you feel the way you do. Think about what the person you are communicating with is feeling and why he feels the way he does. Look beyond emotional reactions, and search for the underlying causes of those emotional reactions. Try to avoid communicating your emotional reactions, and focus on communicating the underlying reasons for your emotional reactions.

When speaking to individuals who are emotional, give them an opportunity to calm down before continuing the communication. Then talk to them about what they are feeling and why they feel the way they do. Never ignore, avoid, or try to gloss over what others are feeling. It won't work. That will never lead to truly effective communication. Try to understand why they are feeling the way they do. Let them know that you care about how they feel. Then work with them in a joint effort to address the needs of all involved parties in a way that recognizes and, if possible, satisfies all or most of those needs. Effective communication is not about simply delivering your thoughts and meeting your needs. Effective communication is about creating true understanding between people who often have competing views. Effective communication requires finding a balance between thinking and feeling, between listening and speaking. It requires respect for and a genuine appreciation of the needs of others.

The Need to Observe and Understand the Nonverbal Cues, Gestures, and Expressions of Others

Not all communication is verbal or even conscious. In fact, a great deal of communication is nonverbal and unconscious. The ability to pick up on the nonverbal cues and unconscious communication of others is, therefore, a critically important skill.

People may look at you a certain way in either a conscious or unconscious effort to communicate a message. Some people pick up on these nonverbal communications—they understand what the other person is thinking or feeling—without being told. Others don't pick up on nonverbal cues very well, and some need to be told what the other person is thinking or feeling because they are unable to understand nonverbal cues and gestures.

Successful people often don't need to be told what someone is thinking. They already know. They are alert to the nonverbal cues of others and are able to use that information to their advantage. I try to do this all the time, but I am especially focused on doing this and conscious of my doing this when I play poker. Many of the world's most successful poker players fall into this category. They have a highly developed ability to observe and read people. They analyze their body movements, gestures, betting patterns, eye contact, facial expressions, posture, and even their heart rates and breathing patterns.

While mastering the ability to observe and interpret the nonverbal and unconscious communications of others is not necessary for success, being unaware of these forms of communication and/or unskilled in analyzing and understanding them can increase your likelihood of failure. For example, assume you are sitting in your cubicle, and as your supervisor passes by, she stops to notice something you are doing or have done. It could be that she sees a risqué or arguably questionable photo you have placed on your desk. It could be she sees you laughing while texting on your cell phone. It could be she sees you brushing your hair or applying makeup while at your desk. She doesn't say a word; she just gives you a puzzled look and keeps walking. *Without speaking, she has communicated her concern over or her displeasure with something.* You may not immediately recognize the reason for her displeasure, but you should know from her nonverbal cue that something concerned her. She may believe it is inappropriate to have certain photos in the workplace. She may think you shouldn't be texting friends while at work. She may think that makeup should be applied in the bathroom—not at your desk. She may think that whatever it is that she noticed violates company policy but wants to check before she says anything. Your conduct may simply offend her personally.

Successful people will not wait to be told what the problem is. They will pick up on the subtle, nonverbal cue (the supervisor's puzzled look) that a problem exists, try to determine the cause of the problem without further communication being required, and correct the problem immediately. Less successful people will either fail to recognize the subtle cue or decide that they don't need to take corrective action unless and until they are told to do so. You are continuously surrounded by nonverbal cues. Look for them like you would look for opportunities, and when you are comfortable that you are interpreting them correctly, trust your instincts and act on them. That comfort level that you feel but can't fully explain is your unconscious mind confirming your read and telling you you're probably correct.

In *Subliminal: How Your Unconscious Mind Rules Your Behavior,* Leonard Mlodinow takes readers on an amazing tour through the latest developments in neuroscience. He says, "With modern instruments, we can now watch as different structures and substructures in the brain generate feelings and emotions. We can measure the electrical output of individual neurons. We can map the neural activity that forms a person's thoughts." Mlodinow tells us: "Human behavior is the product of an endless stream of perceptions, feelings, and thoughts, at both the conscious and the unconscious levels." Conscious thought is what we use when we focus our attention on a task, such as designing a car or solving a math problem. Unconscious thought is what our minds rely upon to recognize and avoid danger or to perform a variety of routine, yet highly complicated tasks. Mlodinow explains,

> The human sensory system sends the brain about 11 million bits of information each second. Our conscious minds cannot process that amount of information. The amount of information that our conscious mind can process has been estimated to be between 16 and 50 bits per second. Although we don't realize it, our brains make many decisions each second. Most of these decisions are unconscious.

According to Mlodinow,

> Evolution has provided us with an unconscious mind because our unconscious is what allows us to survive in a world requiring such massive information intake and processing. Our sensory perception, our memory recall, our everyday decisions, judgements, and activities all seem effortless—but that is only because the effort they demand is expended mainly in parts of the brain that function outside our awareness.

One of the most important functions of your unconscious is the processing of data delivery by your eyes. About one-third of your brain is devoted to processing vision, interpreting color, detecting edges and motion, perceiving depth and distance, identifying objects and faces—and all of that unconscious brain activity proceeds outside of your awareness.

Mlodinow says,

> We look to faces to quickly judge whether someone is happy or sad, content or dissatisfied, friendly or dangerous. And our honest reactions to events are reflected in facial expressions controlled in large part by our unconscious minds. Expressions are a key way we communicate and are difficult to suppress or fake.

In fact, facial expressions are such an important part of how we communicate that there is a discrete part of the brain that is used to analyze faces. It's called the "fusiform face area."

We can tell within a matter of seconds how someone feels by the expression on his or her face. How people move their bodies; their posture; how they position their heads, shoulders, arms, hands, legs, and feet; how their eyes, mouths, fingers, and toes move; whether their eyes' pupils are dilated or contracted—are all examples of unconscious signals that can reveal inner emotions, attitudes, or moods that they may prefer to conceal. These involuntary, nonverbal signals tell an observer more about our state of being, including our attitudes, emotions, thoughts, and feelings, than any words we can say.

Your unconscious mind will pick up on many of these cues. Evolution has caused our brains to develop this unconscious ability for survival. But if you're observant, if you focus your attention on these areas with your conscious mind, you can identify subtle gestures that convey a feeling or transmit a thought. If you pay close attention, you can identify gestures and expressions that reveal a person's inner feelings at that moment. Learning how to interpret nonverbal language—including how gestures, actions, and expressions reveal thoughts, attitudes, and emotions—can give you a much more accurate understanding of people.

In the 1970s, Paul Ekman and W. V. Friesen developed the Facial Action Coding System (FACS) to measure, describe, and interpret facial behaviors. This instrument is designed to measure even the slightest facial muscle contractions and determine what category or categories each facial action fits into. It can detect what the naked eye can't and is used by law enforcement agencies, film animators, and researchers of human behavior.

According to a study conducted by Albert Mehrabian of the University of California, Los Angeles, 55 percent of the emotional messages conveyed in face-to-face communication result from body language. Mehrabian's study found that when an incongruity exists between the spoken word and how you deliver it, 7 percent of the message is conveyed through your words, 38 percent is revealed through your vocal quality, and 55 percent comes through your gestures, expression, and posture. How we communicate is inseparable from the feelings we project, consciously or not.

It is therefore essential that we recognize the importance of nonverbal communication and the role of our unconscious mind in understanding, processing, and communicating information. It is equally important that we consciously work to improve our ability to observe, identify, and interpret the nonverbal and unconscious communication of others. Be alert to all the nonverbal cues that people around you are sending. Don't wait for people to tell you verbally what they want when they have already told you nonverbally.

CHAPTER EIGHT

How Committed Are You to Succeeding?

Lebron James, of the Cleveland Cavaliers, said, "Commitment is a big part of what I am and what I believe. How committed are you to winning? How committed are you to being a good friend? To being trustworthy? To being successful? How committed are you to being a good father, a good teammate, a good role model?"

What Is Commitment?

Being committed means doing whatever it takes. Real commitment requires discipline, courage, sacrifice, and perseverance. Being committed isn't easy. It takes time and effort. Elon Musk, founder of Tesla and Space X, says,

> Work like hell. I mean you just have to put in 80 to 100 hour weeks every week. This improves the odds of success. If other people are putting in 40-hour workweeks and you're putting in 100-hour workweeks, then even if you're doing the same thing you will achieve in four months what it takes them a year to achieve.

Commitment always involves choice and intent. Commitment is never random or accidental. True commitment also demands passion. Without passion our actions lack urgency and intensity. Commitment is also tied to integrity. Our commitment demonstrates our integrity and our integrity often motivates and drives our commitment. Commitments are critical, especially in a team environment, where each team member needs to be able to depend on their teammates to achieve the team's goals.

Making a commitment should never be taken lightly. Many of the things we want won't come quickly or easily. These things require commitment. Saving a down-payment for a car or a house, losing weight, getting a promotion, entering a new profession, maintaining an important relationship, staying married, all of these goals require commitment.

How Do You Know When You're Committed?

Doing what's expected of you in your job, being punctual and prepared, dressing and grooming appropriately, and respecting workplace policies—all show professionalism. Going beyond what's expected by putting in extra hours, bringing energy and initiative to your job every day, helping others, making significant contributions to any group task, keeping yourself and others motivated or taking a leadership role goes beyond professionalism. It shows dedication and commitment.

Do you show up motivated every day? Are you dedicated and ready to learn? Do you listen and take instructions? Do you accept and never argue with feedback? Do you understand that you do not have all the answers? Do you have the courage to admit your mistakes? Do you truly want to learn more from and about your job? If you answered each of these questions with a yes, then you're committed.

The Importance of a Sense of Urgency

Speed has always been an asset. In ancient times, it may have allowed you to run from a wild animal or warn your village of an impending attack. Today, it may allow you to build, grow or save your business. Time is money. Yet, few employees seem to grasp this concept intuitively. We see the absence of a sense of urgency in virtually every workplace.

How often have you been on a lunch break, concerned that you have limited time? You go to a "quick service" restaurant to save time. Unfortunately, the service is anything but quick. As you're standing in a long line, waiting to order, you notice that the cashier is moving with glacial speed. Even worse, there are two available registers but the manager is socializing with one of the other workers rather than opening the second register. No one working, at this "quick service" restaurant, is "quick" and you're not getting the "service" you need.

It happens all too often in stores, at the bank, in movie theaters—everywhere! People lack a sense of urgency. They're often slow. Sometimes irritatingly slow. Do you ever notice this? There is no excuse for it. It results from inadequate training on the part of management and a lack of commitment on the part of employees. It's bad for business. Companies lose customers because of it, and people lose jobs when companies lose customers. People want and have a right to expect service from a "service business." If they are not getting that service within a reasonable amount of time, they will leave and take their business elsewhere.

Slow employees cost their employers more in time and money, while providing less value than fast employees. They get less accomplished, and they irritate customers. This can result in lost business, fewer jobs, and even store closures. It can cost you your job.

Time truly is money. Don't waste your time and don't waste other people's time. Train yourself to move quickly without making mistakes. Make moving quickly a priority. Work on improving your speed, the same way you would work on improving any other skill. Practice!

When I was in college, I was literally the fastest walker on campus. I don't know why. I just was. It was noticeable, especially to my girlfriend who I pulled behind me as I flew around campus. I didn't have to try. It came naturally.

Then I spent a summer in Washington, D.C., as an intern for United States Senator Paul Laxalt (R-NV). On my first day working in the Russell Senate Office Building, I was amazed and dismayed to find that I was one not one of the fastest walkers in the building. How could this be? I was a lightning bolt at college. Walking speed had absolutely nothing to do with my job. I'm sure no one thought I walked slowly, but I didn't like watching others rush past me. So I decided to keep up. I pushed myself to walk faster. I actually practiced speed walking. By the time I left, six months later, I was one of the fastest walkers in the building.

I now look back upon that experience and smile. I didn't really need to walk any faster. No one ever told me to do it. Yet, seeing how fast everyone moved sent me a message. The message was, "If everyone on Capitol Hill moves this fast, maybe there is something important about speed. Maybe this is something I should be even better at." I wanted to have all the skill sets required to succeed. I wanted to be the best I could be at everything I did, even if it didn't mean anything to anyone else—it meant something to me. Speed is important in every business. It communicates competency and a sense of urgency. It evidences superior performance. It communicates appreciation and respect.

If you're a cashier, take the time to learn your register. Know it like the back of your hand. Be able to find the keys with your eyes closed. Practice! This is what executive secretaries do. They practice increasing their typing speed until they can type over one hundred words a minute error free. The faster and more accurate they are, the better jobs they attract and the more money they make.

Be conscious of customers and clients that are waiting. Respect their time. Understand that you are in a "service" business and make it your mission to provide fast, error free, exemplary service. If you cannot commit to doing that, get out of the service business. If you're not willing to make that commitment, you simply don't belong in a service business. It's not fair to your employer, your co-workers or your customers. Find a job that you can be passionate about. Find a job where you will be committed to excellence.

If You're Going to Do Something, Do It Well or Don't Do It at All

My dad taught me many things more by deeds than by words. One thing he said really stuck with me. It was one of the most important things he ever told me. He said, "If you're going to do something, do it well or don't do it at all." He didn't sit down with me like a Greek philosopher and impart these words of wisdom in a moment of revelation. He said it while I was washing the dishes. I was 12 years old, and I remember it like it was yesterday. He had asked me to wash the dishes in the sink, so I filled the sink with soap and water and began washing the dishes. He came into the kitchen and calmly pushed me to the side saying, "That's not how you wash dishes. If you're going to do something, do it well or don't do it all." He then proceeded to empty the sink and show me how he wanted it done. He began by washing the empty sink with soap and water to make sure the sink was clean. He then filled one side of the clean sink with hot soapy water. Then he began taking one plate at a time, scraping the food into the garbage disposal, and then washing it in the soapy water before rinsing and stacking it. He repeated this process several times and then looked at me and said, "Get it?" At the time, I didn't think much about it, but over time, it became a guiding principle in my life. I don't know why that resonated with me. But it did. Thirteen years later, I was married and in law school. My new wife and I were in our new apartment, and she was washing the dishes. LOL. Yep, I sure did. I said, "That's not how you wash dishes." I told her the story about my dad and showed her how he had taught me to wash dishes. She smiled, listened, and did it my dad's way. We both intuitively grasped the important concept that my dad had taught me. It wasn't about the dishes; it was about wanting to do things well. We shared that philosophy and still do. She went on to become a district court judge.

Why waste your time doing anything poorly? Performing poorly will ultimately cost you your job, your customers and possibly your business. Conversely, performing well will improve the performance of the business and thereby provide increased job security for you and your co-workers. It may also lead to increased personal and professional opportunities. Exceptional performance shows commitment. It demonstrates leadership potential and normally leads to advancement and additional career opportunities.

My entire career was ultimately built on this simple principle. It touched every aspect of my work, every letter I wrote, every meeting I attended, every appearance I made, every motion I filed. Everything that I produced and every action I took were undertaken with this principle in mind. I knew that regardless of what may come of my life, if I always did my best work, then at least I would know that I did everything I could to succeed. Invariably, each exceptional effort met with success and each success, reinforced by past successes, created a confidence, a character and a reputation that lead to a remarkable career.

In *The Habit of Going the Extra Mile*, author Napoleon Hill describes "going the extra mile" as the rendering of more and better service than anyone expects and giving that service with a positive attitude. He explains the many benefits of this approach. One chief benefit is the fact that it enables you to profit by the law of contrast because the majority of people do not practice the habit. Hill goes on to point out that "going the extra mile" provides the only logical reason for asking for increased compensation. He explains that if an employee performs no more service than what he is being paid to do, then he is receiving all the pay he is entitled to. Instead of asking for a raise, ask your employer how you can do more for the company. By demonstrating such a high level of commitment, you are more likely to attract increased responsibilities and a raise.

The Habit of Going the Extra Mile is a twelve-page essay written by a man some call "the architect of the philosophy of success." Hill spent most of his life studying and writing about the most successful entrepreneurs in American history. His most famous work, *Think and Grow Rich* (1937), is one of the best-selling books of all time. All of his works are well worth reading.

True commitment, regardless of the endeavor, is absolutely essential not only to the business you work for, but to your personal success as well. Commitment can be declared by words, but evidence of commitment can only be found in your actions.

As Andrew Carnegie, American industrialist and philanthropist, observed, "*As I get older, I pay less attention to what men say. I just watch what they do.*" In whatever you do, be committed.

CHAPTER NINE

Why Courage Is Critical and How to Develop It

W INSTON CHURCHILL, PRIME MINISTER of England from 1940 to 1945 and again from 1951 to 1955, once said, "Courage is rightly considered the foremost of virtues, for upon it, all others depend."

What Is Courage?

Courage shows itself in many forms. We saw it on September 11, 2001, when a group of passengers on United Flight 93 acted to overpower hijackers. We saw it on August 21, 2015, when Anthony Sadler, Spencer Stone, and Alek Skarlatos overpowered a terrorist aboard a high-speed train to Paris. We see it every day when firefighters run into burning buildings and police officers take on armed criminals.

We see it in the story of Jacklyn Lucas, who signed up for the Marines during WWII at the age of 14. He was patrolling Iwo Jima ravines when the Japanese attacked, throwing two grenades directly onto his position. He grabbed one grenade, laid himself over it, and then grabbed a second grenade and pulled it underneath himself as well. He did it to save his comrades. He did it instinctively. It was part of his character. Lucas somehow survived. He needed twenty-six surgeries and retained 250 pieces of shrapnel for the rest of his life. He was awarded the Medal of Honor by President Harry Truman.

I offer you this example not because I expect you to fall on a grenade, but because if this young man could summon the courage to do what he did, it demonstrates that you are more than capable of showing the courage required to deal with virtually any challenge life may present you. These are extraordinary acts of courage. Most of us perform more courageously than we may realize every day. In fact, there are many opportunities for each of us to act with courage on a much more frequent basis.

Karina Sanchez had an extremely difficult home life. At 17, she left home and decided to try her luck being on her own without a place to live. Determined to succeed, she went to school all day. She studied at the public library after school and then went back to her school after the school had closed. She took cardboard out of the recycling dumpster and slept on it at night behind the school until she heard the janitors come in the next morning. Every day, she got up and did it all over again. She graduated in the top 10 percent of her class and received a full scholarship to the University of Denver. Sanchez now owns her own home and has a beautiful daughter. She also runs an after-school program for at-risk kids.

Recently, at McCarran International Airport in Las Vegas, Nevada, I saw a man exit the passenger seat of a vehicle to assist an arriving passenger load her bags into the back of the vehicle. What I found remarkable about this incident was that the man had no hands and no legs. He climbed out of the vehicle on his prosthetic legs and used his arms, without hands, to lift the woman's bag. I can't imagine what my mental state would be if I lost my hands and my legs, but I pray that I would have this man's courage. More than 1,500 Americans have lost a leg or arm in combat in Iraq or Afghanistan, and hundreds have suffered the amputation of multiple limbs. To move forward with their lives, these men and woman must summon incredible courage. They should be an inspiration to all of us. They are amazingly courageous people. They deserve not only our gratitude—they deserve our admiration and respect. They've earned it.

I recently lost a friend named Mark Scott. He had a difficult home life and was on his own at an early age. He discovered coin collecting as a young man and learned that if he could "buy right" and sell at a profit, he would have a business. He ultimately made a fortune, building a business that he was passionate about. Then, just as he was about to slow down and enjoy the fruits of his labor, he got cancer. Mark died eight months after his diagnosis. The eight months that followed his death sentence were filled with chemotherapy, back surgery, and pain. Yet he was a towering inspiration throughout. He never once complained. His courage was truly remarkable.

When others can face tragedy and death with dignity, hope, and grace, how can any of us not summon the courage required for the challenges that we face? These are just a few of the millions of people who show tremendous courage every day. Thinking about the challenges faced by others can really help us put our own challenges into perspective.

It takes courage to overcome ignorance, poverty, and discrimination. It takes courage to walk down the street in an unsafe neighborhood or say "no" to a friend who asks you to try a drug. It takes courage to express what you believe will be an unpopular opinion, to live in an abusive home, to deal with a dysfunctional or alcoholic parent, or to stick up for someone who is being bullied. It takes courage to apply for a job and risk rejection, to express emotions openly, to resist peer pressure, to avoid poor choices, and to fight an addiction to alcohol or drugs. In many cases, it takes courage just to make it through the day. The starting point to overcoming our fears and developing courage is to look at the factors that cause us to be fearful.

Understanding Your Fears

For many of us, fears come from our childhoods. We become preoccupied with the idea of failing. We become hypersensitive to the opinions of others. Fears can paralyze us. They can stop us from taking the action necessary to realize our dreams. We hesitate. We procrastinate. We delay. We become indecisive. We make excuses and find reasons not to move ahead.

Fears can be caused by ignorance. When we have limited information, we are less likely to act. We fear change. We fear the unknown.

The act of gathering information about a particular subject can cause us to become more courageous and confident. The courageous person is not fearless. Courageous people control their fears rather than allowing their fears to control them.

Failure to confront your fears can allow them to increase and eventually take control of your life. As your fears increase, your self-respect and self-confidence diminish. When you confront your fears, your self-respect and self-confidence grow.

Some people fear rejection. They are obsessed with how they appear to others and have trouble taking independent action. Some even fear success. They may crave the attention they get by being helpless victims and fear losing that attention and support if they make progress and appear more secure and self-sufficient.

By objectively analyzing your fears, you can begin the process of eliminating them. You begin eliminating your fears and developing courage by taking actions that are consistent with courage and self-confidence and by resolving not to be driven by your fears.

Understanding Failure

From an early age, we are taught to fear failure. The truth is that failure is a natural part of innovation. Work tirelessly, persist, pivot, and persevere, but never fear failure. Steve Jobs, founder of Apple Computer said, *"Failure can be the greatest thing in our lives."* Many of the most successful people in history have experienced and had to overcome multiple failures. Michael Jordan was cut from his high school team. Here's what Jordan has to say about failure:

> I have missed more than 9,000 shots in my career. I have lost almost 300 games. On 26 occasions I have been entrusted to take the game winning shot, and I missed. I have failed over and over and over again in my life. And that is why I succeed.

Here are a few other examples of well-known people who have overcome failure:

+ Walt Disney was fired from the newspaper where he worked because he was considered to have no imagination or good ideas.

+ Thomas Edison created more than one thousand inventions and is said to have failed ten thousand times before inventing the light bulb.

+ Oprah Winfrey was told that she was unfit for TV and was fired from her job as a TV reporter.

+ J. K. Rowling's first Harry Potter book was rejected by twelve publishers.

All of these people have at least three things in common: 1) They had the courage to reach for success, 2) they failed, and 3) they persevered until they achieved success.

On August 4, 2009, Brian Action, founder of WhatsApp, tweeted, "Facebook turned me down. It was a great opportunity to connect with some fantastic people. Looking forward to the next adventure." On February 20, 2014, four and a half years later, Facebook bought WhatsApp for $19 billion. It doesn't matter how many times you fail. What matters is your dedication and commitment to success. See each failure as an opportunity to learn, make adjustments, and keep trying.

Joe Kraus, cofounder of Excite and partner at Google Ventures, says,

> The people that thread the line between vision and being able to execute, have this healthy fear of failing that drives them. It does not paralyze them, but drives them to be more persistent—to work harder than the next person. That's a magic formula.

Do not interpret failure as a sign of weakness, but as an integral part of the learning process. Failure gives us valuable feedback on what we need to work on next. You need to see each failure as a learning experience, analyze your failures, learn from them, and make appropriate adjustments.

If you're not failing, you're not trying. You're not reaching, and you're not growing. In everything you do, every time you have the courage to try something new, you will succeed or you will fail and learn from that experience. Both add value to your life.

One of my favorite quotes comes from Robert F. Kennedy, who said, "*Only those who dare to fail greatly can ever hope to achieve greatly.*" Success requires a willingness to fail. You can't have success without it. Most successful businesspeople have experienced a good deal of failure. In fact, their success often comes from what they learned from their failures. I have learned much more from my failures than I have from any of my successes. Failure is, by far, the superior teacher.

I have failed repeatedly. Many times. I'll share two of my failures with you and tell you what I learned from them. I had been president of the Consolidated Students of the University of Nevada, while attending UNLV. When I was in law school, at the University of San Diego School of Law, I ran for student body president. I lost by twenty votes. I went home and cried. I felt devastated. A week later, a friend suggested that I run for president of the American Bar Association, Law School Division. I wasn't even a member of the ABA/LSD at the time. I flew to St. Petersburg, Florida, and joined the ABA/LSD the same day I ran for president of the organization. Bold move—an understatement. Another law student, who was the ninth circuit governor of the ABA/LSD at that time, was the only other person running for the position, and I was the only law student in the United States to challenge him. The winner would be decided by a vote of his colleagues, the fifteen current ABA/LSD governors. After we had both been afforded an opportunity to meet with all of the governors, a vote was taken. I lost by one vote. What I learned from that experience was that it doesn't matter if you win or lose. What really matters is that you have the courage to make the effort. Win or lose—you are enriched by the experience.

While I was in law school and working as an intern for a San Diego law firm, I conceived the idea for a board game called Notable Quotables. I spent the next five years collecting contemporary quotes for the game in my spare time. I met with a magazine distributor who gave me hundreds of copies of free, coverless magazines that were bound for incineration. Every week, I would read all of these magazines looking for funny, inspiring, witty, or sensational quotes. I made a deal with the law firm I was working for to allow me to use the firm's word processing staff to transcribe all the quotes. I raised $1 million so that I could hire top designers, plastic manufacturers, and printers to design and produce the game. Notable Quotables arrived in San Diego stores on November 29, 1990. During the next 25 days, 4,627 games were sold. One Nordstrom department store sold 276 games in one day, and Diane Peacor, the Nordstrom store manager, was quoted as saying, "Our switchboard was jammed with calls for Notable Quotables."

Every television station, radio station, and newspaper in San Diego was talking about the game. Notable Quotables sold more games in its first month than Trivial Pursuit or Pictionary sold when their independent inventors first released them. Ultimately, both of those historic games were licensed by larger companies and became huge successes. I tried to follow that business model. After three years of independently promoting Notable Quotables, I eventually licensed it to a company whose founder had an incredible track record. He was one of the salesmen who launched Trivial Pursuit and one of the founders of the Games Gang, which launched Pictionary. I spent months negotiating my contract with him. We agreed to a deal. We had a written contract. Unfortunately, he failed to honor that contract, and it killed the game. Three years of effort were destroyed. I won our arbitration for breach of contract and was awarded hundreds of thousands in damages, which I returned to my investors, but the game was now yesterday's news.

That three-year odyssey was the equivalent for me of a real-world MBA. While promoting Notable Quotables, I worked 16-hour days and, to save money, I never hired a permanent employee. Each of those three years I flew back from the New York Toy Fair. Each time the plane landed, I was a ball of sweat, on oxygen, and taken from the plane by ambulance to the hospital for fatigue and pneumonia. On my third flight home from the New York Toy Fair, immediately after boarding the plane, I wrote my Last Will and Testament out by hand because I was convinced that I would not survive the flight home.

Not long after that flight, I was asked to lecture to an MBA class at the University of San Diego. I told the class that I would succeed with the game or "die trying." At that time, I was actually willing to die rather than fail and lose my investors' money. After the lecture, the professor of the class said something that made me stop and listen to reason. He said, "Mr. Chanos, I want you to think about something: If you die, the game will fail." Those wise words reached me and gave me permission to slow down. He probably saved my life.

This failure had a profound impact on me. It taught me so much about what not to do. It taught me that even when you have a great idea, intelligence, a strong work ethic, core values, and adequate capitalization, you might still fail. It taught me that maintaining my health was essential to achieving success. It taught me to hire and surround myself with the best people I could find. It taught me to plan ahead and anticipate challenges. It taught me how to launch a consumer product and how to deal with and overcome a seemingly never-ending cascade of obstacles that are inherent in every entrepreneurial endeavor. It taught me that by choosing my investors wisely and keeping them fully informed, they would continue to believe in and support me, even when confronted with failure. And the most painful yet valuable lesson I learned: To some people, contracts are nothing but insignificant pieces of paper— the character of the people you do business with is what truly counts. Those three years enriched my life in ways that I may never fully realize.

The Capacity for Courage and How to Develop It

The capacity for courage lies within all of us, and there are ways to increase it. The ability to control fear and boost your willingness to act is a skill that can be cultivated and acquired. Acting with courage more consciously and more often can be a great source of fulfillment and satisfaction. What would you dare to dream, to be, to do, to try, or to say if you had the courage to overcome your fears? When we develop the habit of courage, a new world of possibilities opens up to us.

The first step is the most important step. You need to be willing to move out of your comfort zone with no guarantee of success. *Action is magic!* You cannot create change in your life without taking action. You must summon the courage to take action. One way to get the courage to begin is to plan thoroughly in advance. Set clear goals and objectives. Gather information. Read and do research. Prepare a plan of action, and then take that important first step. With each success, your confidence and courage will build, and your fears will diminish.

Simply by attempting to develop courage you will begin to set more challenging and exciting goals for yourself. You will have the confidence of knowing that you can achieve your goals. You will be able to face every situation with a self-confidence born out of having overcome your fears. You will have conquered your fears and developed courage. It's true. It actually works. How do I know? Because I do it. Try it.

CHAPTER TEN

Is Your Attitude an Asset or a Liability?

THERE IS AN OLD saying: "Attitude is everything." The last fifteen years have provided all of us with more than sufficient justification for pessimism and cynicism.

American troops in Iraq and Afghanistan; Hurricane Katrina; billions in bank bailouts; gun violence; threats from ISIS, Iran, Syria, North Korea, Russia, and China; racial tensions and divisions; failures in immigration and health care reform; unprecedented levels of student debt; increasing unemployment and income inequality; political dysfunction and paralysis.

Americans are witnessing what seems like a never-ending stream of institutional failures. Total financial losses to the U.S. economy caused by the 2008 financial crisis have been estimated at $22 trillion. Millennials are realizing that what may have worked for their parents does not necessarily work for them.

Ezra Klein, who started the news site Vox.com, says,

> The last fifteen years are a story of severe institutional failure that should profoundly concern people. I don't think you can look at this period and feel confident in our institutions or their ability to make wise decisions or handle emergencies effectively.

Institutional failures over the past fifteen years can't help but have a profound effect on people's attitudes, and we know from experience that people's attitudes have a profound effect on their performances.

Therefore, we must learn how to understand and control our attitudes in order to achieve our objectives.

Attitude Is Everything

Thomas Jefferson, the third president of the United States, once said, "Nothing can stop the man with the right mental attitude from achieving his goals. Nothing on earth can help the man with the wrong mental attitude." Each of us is influenced by the events that shape our respective environments. Each of us also encounters difficult events in our lives that impact us on a more personal level.

We may have had to endure physical or emotional pain. The heartaches of someone leaving you, a loved one dying, being in a tragic accident, or being fired from a job—these and other misfortunes can all be extremely painful. Some disappointments are more severe than others. No matter how bad you think your experiences may be, always remember that many people face challenges and disappointments that are far worse than yours. They are able to cope with those challenges with dignity, courage, and grace. Nothing is as bad as it may first seem. You can and will overcome whatever challenges you may face.

Even more important is the need to reflect back upon the discussion of choice. Life is about choices. It is not what happens to you that matters. It's how you choose to respond. How you choose to think about it. How you choose to allow it to affect you. These are the things that matter, and they are entirely within your control.

Why Is a Positive Attitude So Important?

Attitude determines everything else in our lives! Our attitudes affect all of our relationships. Our attitudes affect our careers, our emotional well-being, our decisions, our actions, and our influence on others. Our attitudes and mindsets affect every aspect of our lives.

Your thoughts become your words. Your words become your actions. Your actions become your habits. Your habits become your character, and your character becomes your destiny. Your attitude will either draw people to you, or it will repel them.

A significant percentage of Americans have cynical leanings. They mistrust or are skeptical about virtually everything and everyone: government, big business, the products they purchase, and authority figures. A positive attitude doesn't guarantee success, but an overly cynical attitude can guarantee failure. While a healthy degree of cynicism may be useful at times, being overly cynical can be very limiting.

Cynicism can be caused by disappointment. Disappointment often begins with unrealistic expectations. Expecting great things to happen to you with little or no effort on your part will naturally lead to disappointment. Having high expectations for yourself is great, but you must also be prepared to do what it takes to make those expectations a reality.

Attitude Is a Matter of Choice

It takes self-examination to understand the roots of a negative and harmful attitude, but the benefits of improving your attitude will last you a lifetime. Changing your attitude can literally change your life. The wonderful thing about attitude is that it's a matter of choice. It's your choice. You can choose to live every single day of your life with a positive attitude.

Most great athletes, surgeons, artists, and successful businesspeople use positive affirmations and visualizations to enhance focus, and improve their attitudes. They choose to think positive thoughts. They visualize positive results. They create their own positive reality by thinking positively and visualizing their success. They also use exercise and the resulting benefits of weight loss, increased energy, and a sense of accomplishment to improve their attitudes.

A positive attitude is life changing. Enthusiasm is infectious. It communicates commitment and determination. Enthusiasm is one of the most attractive and powerful traits you can possess. Your attitude can become a habit. Do you think and act as if what you want is impossible? If so, that will become your reality.

Choose to be happy. When negative thoughts enter your mind, ignore them. Substitute them with positive thoughts. Choose to be optimistic. Find reasons to smile more often. Have faith in yourself. Control your thoughts instead of allowing them to control you.

Attitude Influences Performance

Some people believe they don't have choices in life. They believe that their fate is out of their hands. They have a passive approach to life. Whatever happens, they think, is beyond their control. Nothing could be further from the truth. According to Stanford University's Carol Dweck, psychologist and author of Mindset: The New Psychology for Success, the attitude that we bring to our creative work and to mentoring can play a huge role in determining how much of our inborn talents are realized.

According to a survey conducted by Dweck while she was at Columbia University, 85 percent of American parents think it is important to tell their kids that they're smart. Dweck and her team at Columbia studied the effects of praise on students in dozens of New York schools. Students were given tests, and then some were praised for their *intelligence* while others were praised for their *effort*. Students were then asked to choose their next set of tests. Dweck's studies found that 90 percent of those praised for their *effort* chose the *harder* follow-up tests. Of those praised for their *intelligence*, a majority chose the *easy* follow-up test. The "smart" kids took the easy path.

If we believe that our talents are incapable of further development, we are effectively dismissing options for growth. In contrast, if we believe that our talents and intelligence continue to evolve as a result of how much effort we put in, the opportunities are endless.

Change Your Attitude, and It Will Change Your Life

Adults in a "fixed mindset" think that great effort, struggle, and failure are signs of weakness. People in a "growth mindset" enjoy the effort, appreciate the struggle, and embrace failure as a learning opportunity. The critical reality is that we are not hostage to some naturally granted level of talent. We can make ourselves what we will. Greatness isn't reserved for a preordained few. It is available to you and to everyone.

You have the power to change your life. Life isn't about what happens to you. It's about what you do about it. If there is anything you want to change in your world, you need to begin by changing your attitude toward it. You need to believe in yourself. Not in some delusional, unrealistic way but in a rational, optimistic, and courageous way that inspires you to action. From there, add determination and commitment, and you will be on your way to realizing your dreams.

You can find at least two ways to look at virtually everything. A pessimist sees difficulty in opportunity, whereas an optimist sees opportunity in difficulty. Choose optimism over cynicism.

Two wonderful books on this subject are *The Power of Positive Thinking*, by Norman Vincent Peale, and *Success through a Positive Mental Attitude*, by Napoleon Hill and W. Clement Stone. These books underscore the basic idea that success and fulfillment in life begin with your thoughts.

CHAPTER ELEVEN

Choosing the Right Career Path

IN ORDER FOR PEOPLE to become productive members of society, they need jobs. Ideally, they need careers. Yet finding a job or a career can often be a daunting task. Moreover, finding employment and succeeding in the workplace are virtually impossible for individuals who do not adopt and practice the core values discussed in this book. Employers need employees who understand and act upon these core values. Yet, many young people may never have been taught or fail to act upon these core values. If you really want to become successful, you must embrace these core values. It's not optional. It's absolutely essential.

Whether you are a young person attempting to enter the job market for the first time or someone who is attempting to improve your employment opportunities by securing a new or better job, your understanding and adoption of the core values, also referred to as character traits in Chapter Six of this book, will be absolutely critical to your success. Understanding and accepting these values are essential first steps in reaching your personal and professional goals. Once you have accepted these core values and started to live your life based on these values, the next steps are choosing and then embarking upon the right career path.

Gather Information about Career Options

Before choosing your career, research your career options by accessing community resources and planning your approach. Use the Internet, schools' career counselors, or social service agencies to identify and access your communities' career resources. Most communities provide some level of career support.

Types of career support include these:

- *Information*—Information that supports career and learning choices is available over the Internet and through various community agencies. You can also obtain labor market information, such as salaries of various professions, employment rates in various professions, available training programs, and current job openings through your local library.

- *Assessments*—Many career assessment tests rely on both quantitative and qualitative methodologies. Career assessments help individuals identify and better understand their unique interests, personalities, values, and skills to determine how well they may match with a certain career.

- *Counseling*—Career counseling is available through various community agencies, whose skilled professionals can help you to assess your interests, personality, values, and skills, and to explore career options.

Consider Your Interests and Your Abilities

Choose your career wisely. If possible, choose something you think you will love. Or, choose something you have a genuine interest in. You also need to rationally and honestly consider your skills, training, and abilities. You need to be sensible and realistic—but you also need to reach beyond your comfort zone. If you don't have the skills and training you need for a given job or profession, then don't be afraid to take a step back and acquire those skills and that training. You have three options: Enhance your existing abilities before you take on new challenges, choose something that is more in line with your existing abilities, or take a chance and acquire new skills and abilities as you go.

The Jung Typological Test, based on Carl Jung's and Isabel Briggs Myers' typological approach to personality, is available free at HumanMetrics.com (www.humanmetrics.com). It's a fun online, multiple-choice test that you can take in five minutes. It will give you a four-letter personality profile. Mine is ENTJ. The letters stand for each person's most dominant personality characteristics: extroverted (E); intuition (N); thinking (T); judging (J). You can then go to Pinterest (www.pinterest.com)—also for free—and search for information on your four-letter code. Pinterest is a visual discovery tool that you can use to find ideas for all your projects and interests.

The test can provide you with incredible insights into your personality. It is not a perfect test for everyone. Not all people fit neatly into one of the sixteen personality types listed. However, it can provide useful insights to anyone and is well worth taking. Humanmetrics.com also offers additional tests that can allow you to determine what careers may best suit your personality.

Rasmussen College has created an easy, interactive career aptitude test that you can take online for free. Take the Career Aptitude Test from Rasmussen College at http://www.rasmussen.edu/resources /aptitude-test.

Team Technology: Online Business Resources offers the MMDI™ Personality Test, which they describe as the most advanced and meaningful personality test on the Internet, at http://www.teamtechnology .co.uk.

Choose Something That Inspires Your Commitment

What do you "love" to do? Do you love working with children? Consider teaching, coaching, and childcare. Do you love the outdoors? Consider the national or local park services, environmental studies, construction, or landscaping. Do you love working with people? Consider retail, counseling, marketing, or sales. The list is endless. Think about things that are important to you, and then find something that satisfies your needs, interests, or desires.

Consider the lifestyle that you want and how your prospective employment may complement your lifestyle choices. For example, you may want to work from home. You may want a job that gives you the flexibility to leave early so you can pick your kids up from school. You may want to travel and need more vacation time. You may want a job where you can learn new things. You may be interested in starting your own business and decide to learn from an existing business before you branch off on your own.

Consider the culture of the company and the nature of your employer. What are the priorities of the company, and how do those priorities align with your own? Is the company all about profit, or does it care about quality, service, value, and people? Does the organization have a social conscience? Do you like the people you've met in the interview process? Do they seem warm and welcoming? Would you enjoy going to lunch with them? Would you like to spend time with them outside of work? Do you respect them? Can you learn from them? Can you give them your commitment and passion? All of these issues should be considered when searching for a job that you love—a job that you can and will be excited about—a job that will inspire your commitment and dedication.

Analyzing Your Options

In considering your employment and career options, you first need to determine what goals are important to you:

+ Gaining status, wealth, position, or power?

+ Pleasing, satisfying, or impressing someone other than yourself: perhaps your parents, a spouse, or a love interest, classmates, colleagues or friends, the views of society in general?

+ Having enough time for your family, the flexibility to work from home, the ability to get time off for travel?

+ Having a real passion for your work, doing something you love, desiring to learn or desiring to help others?

You need to begin your analysis by examining and understanding your motivations and your priorities. The next things you will want to learn: What are the critical tasks or key responsibilities of a given job or career that you are considering? What skills will be required to excel at those tasks and successfully discharge those responsibilities?

What specific skills do you have that will allow you to succeed in fulfilling the responsibilities that are likely to be expected of you? What are your strengths (existing skills that will help you excel in a position), and what are your weaknesses (required skills that you lack)? If you lack the skills required to succeed in a specific job or profession, then pursuing that job or profession at this time may not be the right choice for you.

There is no point in pursuing a job, trade, or career when you lack the skills required to succeed. A better decision might be to take a step back and acquire those skills before attempting to secure such a position. Or, you could choose a different job, trade, or career that is more closely aligned with your existing skill set. Alternatively, you could choose to get a job in a field related to your top choice and take classes online or at a nearby college to start working on the necessary skill set or degree requirements.

You don't need to have perfected all the skills required for a given position before seeking out that position. Your skills can and will develop on the job. But you will increase your chances of success, if you have a strong aptitude and above average competency in the field prior to seeking the position.

Table 1 on pages 112-113 contains a list of skills that are commonly required in order to excel at various jobs and professions. Rank yourself, on a scale of 1–10 (with 1 as the lowest skill level and 10 as the highest skill level) on each of the skills. Then identify the skills that you believe will be required to excel at a given position.

Do some research to confirm your assumptions concerning what skills are likely to be required for a given employment position. When you find a match, between your skill set and the skills required of a given position, you will have identified a job, trade or career where you are likely to find success. This is important, because you are far more likely to be happy in a job or profession where you can and will excel.

Proficiency in one or more of the skills listed in Table 1 is typically required for most jobs and professions. The exact skill set required will depend on the position. How would you rank yourself (in comparison to your peers or those that you are likely to be competing with) on the skills listed in the table?

TABLE 1. Evaluate your skill set

Skill	Description
Leadership skills	The ability to motivate and lead others
Judgment skills	The ability to make good decisions
Organizational skills	The ability to organize people and tasks
Management skills	The ability to manage others
Strategic skills	The ability to see the big picture and think strategically
Motivational skills	The ability to inspire and motivate others
Relationship skills	The ability to work with others and build consensus
Communication skills	The ability to communicate effectively
Teaching skills	The ability to teach and transfer concepts and skills
Coaching skills	The ability to improve the performance of others
Delegation skills	The ability to assign and manage tasks
Supervision skills	The ability to supervise others
Financial skills	The ability to read, understand and use financial information
Accounting skills	The ability to manage and report financial information
Observational skills	The ability to observe things that others might overlook
Listening skills	The ability to hear and process what others are saying
Negotiating skills	The ability to negotiate successfully
Dispute resolution skills	The ability to negotiate successfully
Analytical skills	The ability to resolve conflicts
Writing skills	The ability to write clearly and succinctly

Source: Created by author.

Table 1. Evaluate your skill set (cont'd)

Skill	Description
Public speaking skills	The ability to confidently and competently address an audience
Social media skills	The ability to leverage social media
Networking skills	The ability to reach others and expand networks of communication
Social skills	The ability to attract and work with others
Marketing skills	The ability to promote a product or service
Creative skills	The ability to design, create or innovate
Graphic skills	The ability to produce powerful visuals
Design skills	The ability to create and design deliverables
Computer skills	Proficiency with computers, programs and technology
Sales skills	The ability to sell products or services
Physical ability	The ability to perform physical activities
Language skills	The ability to communicate in multiple languages
Technology skills	A thorough understanding of computers, networks, and programs
Technical skills	A thorough understanding of technology and/or machines
Typing skills	The ability to type fast and error free

Source: Created by author.

Remember, if you lack the skills required for a certain position, you always have the ability to learn, improve, or perfect those skills before seeking that position. Establish your bench mark, that is, figure out exactly what educational degrees and skills are required by those who hire people in your chosen profession. How would you evaluate your skill set today?

After assessing your skill set, consider the skills required of various positions and decide where you are most likely to find success. Then consider how those positions might meet your overall goals, priorities, and objectives. This should allow you to narrow down the choices that are most likely to be a good fit for you—choices that can lead to a happy, successful, and meaningful life.

Finally, consider other intangible issues that are likely to influence your satisfaction with the position you are considering. How do you feel about the people you would be working with? How do you and your family feel about the city you would be working and living in? What is the cost of living in that community? What is the community's median home price? How do you and your family feel about where your children would be attending school? What level of compensation and benefits come with the position? Are you motivated and excited about the position? Do you have a real passion for the work? Do you agree with the mission of the company? Would the company assist you with (or provide time off for) additional educational or training opportunities as you move forward? Based on all of these considerations, you should be able to make a good, well-considered decision.

Network with Others to Expand Your Opportunities

Leverage your relationships for job referrals, recommendations, and/ or introductions. If you don't have relationships with individuals who can mentor you or give you advice, get involved in your community and work to develop helpful relationships, referrals, and recommendations. If you're already employed—join industry groups, attend conferences, volunteer at your children's school, or offer your volunteer services to nonprofits. Try to meet new people. Set a goal for yourself of trying to meet one new person every day.

If this seems too ambitious, try to meet at least one or two new people every week. Look for opportunities at school, at your job, at the grocery store, at the car wash, at the mall—wherever you happen to be. Introduce yourself to new people. Your instincts will tell you when it's the right time.

Start by simply being open to people and to opportunities when they present themselves. Be friendly, warm, respectful, and inviting when you meet new people. Say "hello" to people, and make it easy for them to say hello to you. Don't be afraid of rejection. Have courage and confidence. Don't expect every encounter to be positive or instantly lead to a new friendship. Good things take time and effort. Invest the time. Make the effort. Radiate a warm, positive, and authentic personality. Carry a genuine and compassionate confidence rather than a boastful or contrived confidence. Let your positive, authentic personality act like a magnet of attraction.

Even if you only meet one new person each week, you will have made over fifty new contacts over the course of a year. You never know what those new relationships may lead to or how they may improve your life. People you say hello to may simply be impressed by your attitude. They may be looking for an employee or a partner just like you. Who knows? If you make a good impression, it may lead to an incredible opportunity. You never know where a chance encounter may lead. I am always looking for talented people who can add value to the businesses I am involved with or whose talents and skills may present new opportunities. So are many other employers and businesspeople. Great people are hard to find. Be one of them and don't be hard to find. Get out there and get noticed!

Sincerity screams. So be sincere. Be yourself. Be real. Most importantly, if you do get an opportunity, perform at your highest level. Reward those who believe in you by being worthy. Seek out people you believe may be able to help you, and try to make new connections. Never overlook people you believe can do nothing for you. You may be surprised. Some of my greatest successes in life can be traced to introductions from people I never would have imagined might play an important role in my life. You never know when opportunity will knock on your door. You need to hear it knocking. You need to answer the door. And you need to be ready to make the most of it when it does present itself.

Think about opportunity this way:

Knock, Knock

Who's there?

Opportunity.

Opportunity Who?

Opportunity Lost!

OR

Knock, Knock

Who's there?

Opportunity.

Great! I've been expecting you.

Opportunity seized!

Failure to recognize opportunities when they present themselves can result in lost opportunities. You need to be constantly looking for opportunities—and not only recognize them when they present themselves but seize them. I believe that opportunities come to all of us. Some people recognize opportunities for what they are and take advantage of them. Others are less alert or unprepared. They are presented with opportunities, but fail to recognize them or fail to capitalize on them. Be alert to opportunities, be prepared to take advantage of them when they do present themselves, and make the most of them.

Always treat everyone with kindness and respect. A seemingly insignificant stranger may later become someone who changes your life forever. By expanding your network of contacts, you expand your potential for new opportunities. Networks are not just about who can help you today. Networks can and should last a lifetime.

Technology platforms like LinkedIn and Facebook can be invaluable in developing and maintaining networks. Think about how you are using these platforms and how you are presenting yourself on these platforms. Becoming visible is an important part of networking. Create visibility for yourself in person by attending events and electronically by posting information, writing a blog, commenting on a post, or asking a question. In all instances, make certain that the visibility you create places you in a favorable light. Your career options will be enhanced by meeting new people, making the right choices, exhibiting character, having courage, communicating effectively, and being committed.

Chapter Twelve

How to Negotiate Successfully

W E ALL NEGOTIATE EVERY day. We negotiate with our parents, children, spouses, friends, merchants, service providers, employers, and countless others. Everyone negotiates, some more effectively than others. Negotiating is a skill. The better you are at it, the more successful you will be.

In 1995 and again in 1996, I participated in the Harvard Negotiation Project. I also had the privilege of negotiating directly with Harvard Professor Roger Fisher, a giant in the field of negotiation. Roger Fisher and William Ury coauthored *Getting to Yes: Negotiating Agreement Without Giving In*. This is what I learned from that experience.

Most negotiations take the form of positional bargaining. In positional bargaining, the people representing each party state their respective positions on a given issue. The parties then go back and forth to bargain from their respective positions in an attempt to agree on one position. Haggling over the price of an item (a car, a house, or a salary) is a typical example of positional bargaining.

Fisher and Ury argue that what they call "principled negotiation" leads to better, more rationally based, fair, and enduring agreements. Fisher and Ury identify four principles of principled negotiation. The four principles are 1) separate the people from the problem, 2) focus on interests rather than positions, 3) generate a variety of options before settling on an agreement, and 4) insist that the agreement be based on objective criteria.

Separating the People from the Problem

Because most conflicts are based on differing interpretations of the facts, it is crucial for both sides to understand the other's point of view. The parties should try to put themselves in the other side's (the other person's) place. Each side should try to make proposals that would be appealing to the other side.

Emotions are a major source of problems in negotiations. The first step in dealing with emotions is to acknowledge them. Try to understand where your emotions are coming from and why you feel the way you do. Allow the people on the other side to express their emotions. In fact, encourage them to do so. Listen attentively. Give the speaker your full attention, occasionally summarizing the speaker's points to let him/her know you understand. Apologies or an expression of sympathy can be one of the most powerful and cost-effective means of moving an emotionally charged negotiation forward. Think of the other side as your partners in the negotiation rather than as adversaries. Work on improving your relationship with them and separate the human relationship and emotional issues from the facts, the substantive issues of the negotiation.

Focus on Interests

Good agreements focus on each party's interests, rather than on their positions. As Fisher and Ury explain, "Your position is something you have decided upon. Your interests are what caused you to so decide." For example, you may want to send your child to college, but you can't afford it. So you go to your employer and ask for a raise. Your underlying "interest" is that you need to be able to help your child pay college tuition. Your "position" is that you need a raise to be able to do that. By disclosing your underlying interest to your employer, you may learn that your employer has a scholarship program that can be used to reduce your child's tuition costs. A raise may not be the only answer or even the best answer. But you might never even consider other and possibly better options, unless you approach the problem by examining and considering solutions that satisfy your underlying "interests". When a problem is defined in terms of each party's underlying interests, it is often possible to find a solution that satisfies everyone's interests.

Identify both parties' interests regarding the issues at hand. This can be done by asking why they hold the positions they do. Try to look beyond their positions and discover their underlying interests. Work on trying to satisfy their interests. Once you understand each other's interests, you can consider various options that may satisfy both parties' interests. You cannot generate options that might satisfy your respective interests if you're only thinking about each other's positions. You need to discover what each other's interests are and then generate options to satisfy those interests.

Generate Options

Parties often decide prematurely on an option to satisfy their needs and fail to consider alternative options. Parties also normally feel that it is up to the other side to come up with a solution that satisfies their own needs. These are common mistakes.

The parties should consider all possible options and solutions that may satisfy their respective interests. Brainstorming sessions should be used to generate options. Wild and creative proposals should be encouraged during these sessions. Only after a variety of proposals have been made should the group turn to evaluating the ideas.

The parties should consider shared interests. Fisher and Ury urge, "Look for items that are of low cost to you and high benefit to them, and vice versa."

For example, assume that you are buying a new home, and the seller is asking for $200,000. You attempt to negotiate the purchase price, but the seller won't move off the $200,000 price. They tell you that the price is firm. Why is the price firm? What is the seller's "interest" in refusing to lower the $200,000 selling price? Is the seller a developer? Is this one of many homes in a development that the seller is trying to sell? It may be that the seller needs to establish a minimum $200,000 selling price to create a bench mark for future sales. If they sell a house to you at $180,000 it will be a recorded transaction that other buyers will see. Soon, everyone will want to buy the same houses in this development for $180,000 rather than $200,000.

Therefore, the seller has little if any flexibility on lowering the sales price. In this example, lowering the sales price can actually cost the seller much more than the $20,000 discount you are seeking. By understanding the "interests" that underlie the seller's "position," you can generate options to satisfy the seller's "interests" and still achieve your objective of obtaining a discount. One way to do that, in this instance, would be to tell the seller that you will pay the seller's full purchase price of $200,000, so long as the seller gives you a $20,000 credit toward upgrades in appliances, floorings, and finishes. These are things that are not publicly disclosed and are, therefore, unlikely to impact other transactions in the development. In addition, these are items that have a low cost to the seller (because they buy them in bulk) and a high value to you. By focusing on interests, rather than positions, the parties are more likely to reach an agreement and arrive at a win/win solution.

Identify the decision makers and target proposals directly toward them. Be creative. Don't just rely on the other side to come up with creative options that satisfy their own interests. You need to come up with creative options that may satisfy their interests as well as your own, options that they may not have considered.

I once purchased a three-acre piece of property for $2.5 million. I believed that the location was likely to appreciate (grow in value), and I wanted to purchase the neighboring three-acre piece of property as well, hopefully for the same price. I approached my neighbor and asked him what he wanted for his three-acre property. This is how the negotiation proceeded:

> ME: Hi, my name is George Chanos. I'm interested in purchasing your property. Would you be willing to sell it?

> NEIGHBOR: Sure, I want $10 million.

> ME: Wow! Really? I would never pay that. I just purchased the same-sized property directly next to yours for $2.5 million. How about this? I will sell you my property for $10 million.

> NEIGHBOR: I would never pay $10 million for your property.

> ME: I didn't think so.

It seemed as if we were at an impasse. Many people would have simply assumed that a deal was not possible and given up. I didn't. I said,

> ME: I have an idea. What if you get to decide the price, and I get to decide if I'm the buyer or the seller at the price you decide is fair?
>
> NEIGHBOR: No, I won't sell my property for less than $10 million, and I won't pay $10 million for yours.

Again, it seemed like a deal would not be possible. Finally, I said,

> ME: What if we were to list both of our properties together for $20 million? This would give a potential buyer a larger, more attractive piece of property to build a high-rise development. Together, the two properties would be worth more than they would each be worth individually. Maybe if we work together, we can get $20 million for both. We'll each get $10 million.
>
> NEIGHBOR: You're right. I'll do that if my son, who's a real estate agent, gets to list the property and keep the commission.
>
> ME: Done.

We jointly listed our two properties for $20 million and sold them at that price one year later. By generating options, I closed a successful negotiation and made a great profit. My neighbor and his son also profited. Without that creative effort at option generation, it never would have happened. This was a win/win negotiation.

Use Objective Criteria

The parties should use objective criteria to resolve their differences. Decisions based on reasonable, objective standards make it much easier for the parties to agree. Criteria should be both legitimate and reasonable. Scientific findings, professional standards, or legal precedents are all possible sources of objective criteria. One way to test for objectivity is to ask if both sides would agree to be bound by those standards. The parties may also decide to agree upon a fair procedure for resolving their dispute. For example, children may fairly divide a piece of cake by having one child cut the cake and allowing the other child to decide which piece to take. As noted above, I tried this approach with my neighbor when I suggested that he could name the price and I would get to decide if I wanted to be the buyer or the seller at the price he selected. That approach, although objectively fair, was rejected in that instance. However, I have used this approach successfully in other negotiations.

There are three points to keep in mind when using objective criteria. First, each issue should be approached as a shared search for objective criteria. Ask for the reasoning behind the other party's suggestions. If it's reasonable, you should be willing to consider it. Second, each party should keep an open mind. Be reasonable and be willing to reconsider your position when there is a legitimate reason to do so. Third, while you should always be reasonable, you should never give in to pressure or threats.

No negotiation method can completely overcome differences in power. However, Fisher and Ury suggest ways to protect the weaker party against a poor agreement and to help the weaker party make the most of its assets.

Consider Your Alternatives

If you're the weaker party in a negotiation, you should concentrate on assessing your "best alternative to a negotiated agreement" (BATNA). Authors Fisher and Ury note, "The reason you negotiate is to produce something better than the results you can obtain without negotiating." The weaker party should reject agreements that would leave it worse off than its BATNA. Without a clear idea of your BATNA, you are simply negotiating blindly. Power in a negotiation comes from the ability to walk away from negotiations. Thus, the least interested party, or the party with the stronger BATNA, is the more powerful party in any negotiation. These principles are as applicable to personal negotiations as they are to business negotiations.

Openly Confront Unfair Tactics

Sometimes parties will use unethical or unpleasant tactics in an attempt to gain an advantage in negotiations, such as good guy/bad guy routines by their negotiating team, uncomfortable seating for the other side, making the other side wait in their office for an unreasonable amount of time, or marathon negotiating sessions. The best way to respond to such tactics is to explicitly raise each issue as it arises and to engage in principled negotiation to establish procedural ground rules for the negotiation. Unfair tactics can be made less effective simply by recognizing them for what they are. Explicitly identifying unfair tactics to the offending party will usually put an end to such tactics.

You should also prepare for all negotiations by trying to explore both sides' interests and develop options before the negotiation. You can spend nine hours preparing and one hour negotiating or one hour preparing and nine hours negotiating. The negotiation will be much more productive if you spend adequate time preparing. Your use of the above strategies will serve you well in any negotiation. These strategies can make the difference between a successful negotiation and a failed negotiation—between getting what you want and not getting what you want.

Chapter Thirteen

The Profound Influence of Perception

Wʜᴀᴛ ɪs ʀᴇᴀʟɪᴛʏ? Just because we see something a particular way does not make it reality. The science of perception is a fascinating work in progress. Every moment of our lives, our brains are turning sensory data into what we believe is reality. Yet, there is no provable link between "this is what I see" and "this is what is real." Your brain determines your perception. Different brains perceive things differently.

Our Five Senses Limit Our Perception

As humans, we have no conceivable way of understanding the perceptual world of other creatures. Humans, in general, have five senses that operate within a limited band of reception. For example, we can't hear frequencies that bats and dogs hear. Constrained by our perceptual tools, we have no measure of reality outside of our limited perception.

Stephen Hawking belongs to the camp of physicists who believe that reality exists as a material fact, but he concedes, as did Einstein, that science doesn't claim to know what reality is. Even believing in a fixed reality is an assumption—perhaps the greatest assumption of all time. Einstein called it, "my religion" to denote that this was an article of faith for him. He could not prove that reality exists as a fixed state or material fact.

Other quantum pioneers, like Niels Bohr and Werner Heisenberg, do not share Hawking's and Einstein's faith, declaring that if atoms and molecules had no definite position in time and space and no solidity, then the reality perceived through the five senses has no privileged truth behind it. In other words, the fact that you perceive something doesn't make it real. These scientists suggest that reality may not exist at all as a material fact. What we mistake for reality may simply be a product of our perception—an illusion, nothing more. There is no such thing as provable reality. There is only 'your' version of it, which is essentially your perception.

Every day, scientists are making new discoveries that are forcing them to disregard that which they previously thought was true. The philosopher Thomas Nagel, who has studied how different species view the world, speculates that current notions of evolution "will come to seem laughable in a generation or two."

In labs across the world, research on aging is currently underway with a compound called rapamycin, a hormone called klotho, a protein called GDII and telomeres, the final segments of our DNA. All of this research may lead to significant increases in longevity.

Aubrey de Grey, who founded the SENS Research Foundation, is trying to develop regenerative therapies that can postpone aging, possibly indefinitely. Dr. Grey believes that the first human who will live to be 1000 is probably already alive today. Crazy, right? Or is it?

Stewart Brand is a futurist who says that biotech is accelerating four times faster than digital technology. In Brand's opinion, this means that we will one day be able to bring extinct animals back to life. Brand has said, "We will get woolly mammoths back." Crazy, right? Or is it?

"Singularity" represents a school of thought that hypothesizes that accelerating progress in technologies will cause a runaway effect, wherein artificial intelligence will exceed human intellectual capacity and control, thus radically changing or even ending civilization in an event called "the singularity." The capabilities of such a technology-based intelligence may be impossible for a human to comprehend. The technological singularity is an occurrence beyond which events may become unpredictable or even unfathomable.

Stephen Hawking said in 2014, "Success in creating AI (Artificial Intelligence) would be the biggest event in human history. Unfortunately, it might also be the last, unless we learn how to avoid the risks." Hawking believes that in the coming decades, AI could offer "incalculable benefits and risks" such as "technology outsmarting financial markets, out-inventing human researchers, out-manipulating human leaders, and developing weapons we cannot even understand." Hawking believes that "full development of AI could spell the end of the human race". Elon Musk, founder of Tesla and SpaceX, has referred to AI as "potentially more dangerous than nukes". Bill Gates, founder of Microsoft, has said, "I don't understand why some people are not concerned". Clearly, more should be done to analyze, plan and prepare for "the singularity".

As technology continues to evolve in areas like advanced genomics, biotechnology, nanotechnology, space travel, renewable energy, 3-D printing, cloud computing and the Internet of things, we will gain increased perspectives and our perceptions are certain to undergo radical transformations. We really have no way of knowing how limited and inaccurate our current perceptions may be.

Our Bias, Perspective and Expectations Also Limit Our Perception

Our perception is not only limited by our senses. Our perspectives and our biases also limit it. "We see the world, not as it is, but as we are (Talmud)."

Take war as an example. Is war ever right? Is killing ever right? What if you need to kill an intruder to save your family? Is it right then? Most of us see human life as superior to other forms of life. Is it? Is a human life superior to the life of a majestic polar bear—how about a stray dog? Is President Obama doing a good job or a bad job? Is Edward Snowden a hero or a traitor? How we answer these questions will depend on our perspectives and our biases. It's important to be conscious of your perspectives, your biases and your perception, because if you're not someone else may manipulate them.

Things aren't always what they seem. Companies, marketers, politicians, journalists, employers, even your teachers and professors rely on this fact to make you see things the way they want you to see them. We often confuse perception with reality. We mistake how we understand things for the way they really are. Our thoughts and feelings seem real to us so we conclude that they must be true. They must be reality. What if even our most deeply held beliefs were not true? What if what we think is reality, is not reality at all? We often don't realize how our perceptions cloud reality. It is extremely important to be aware of the effect perception has on our beliefs, and how this influences our conclusions, decisions, behaviors and actions.

The media provides a good example of the influence of bias and perspective on perception. Mark Twain once said, "If you don't read the newspaper you are uninformed. If you do read the newspaper you are misinformed."

Fox News and *The Wall Street Journal* have a conservative bias. Information delivered to Fox viewers and/or WSJ readers, therefore, comes from a conservative perspective. This can affect the perceptions, conclusions, decisions, behaviors and actions of its viewers.

CNBC and *The New York Times* have a liberal bias. They deliver information to their viewers and readers through that liberal prism or perspective.

Think about this. The same news—the same "reality"—delivered, explained and understood in two very different ways. The consequence is that "reality" for a CNBC viewer or a *New York Times* reader, may be very different than "reality" for a *Fox* viewer or a *WSJ* reader. Yet it is the identical objective "reality" that each are reporting on. They are simply reporting on it in a very different way.

So how do we know which is true? How do we know who to watch or read? Watch and read both. Also seek out additional viewpoints and perspectives from multiple online media outlets and publications. Only when you have considered multiple informed perspectives, should you decide what to believe is reality.

When I worked Senator Laxalt, one of my responsibilities was to create what was called the "Friday Report." The "Friday Report" was a compilation of news clippings on important stories that had run in more than a dozen different publications. The Senator would take this report home each weekend to understand how the news of the week was being reported and discussed by a wide range of sources. By doing this, he was able to neutralize biases and have a broad perspective on varying views of local, national and international news. This is not to say that Senator Laxalt was without bias. We all have our biases. He was simply smart enough to realize that knowing all sides, of a given news story, would provide him with a better understanding of the objective reality.

Politicians are actually notorious for their strong biases. Democrats and Republicans see the world through their respective biases and perspectives. Some of this is ideologically driven. Some of it arises out of self-interest in perpetuating their tenure and consolidating their power base. Regardless of their motivations, these biases and perspectives often cloud their perceptions. This can result in their becoming inflexible and entrenched in their positions. This, in turn, can create deadlocks and dysfunction.

We are seeing more of this today than ever before. It is actually a very troubling development that has already had serious negative consequences for our country. It illustrates, perhaps better than any other example, the power of bias, perspective and perception.

Personal relationships provide yet another example of the influence of bias and perspective on perception. Have you ever thought someone you dated was a perfect match, only to later ask yourself, "How could I have ever dated that person?" The reality may have never changed. Instead, what may have changed was simply your perception of that individual. At the beginning of your relationship, you may have seen the person you wanted to see. You may have wanted to be in a relationship. You may have had a strong physical attraction to the person, which blinded you to their other, less desirable, traits. In the end, after the fog lifted, you may have seen the person as they really were. Prior to that, your biases and your perspectives may have influenced your perception.

Our expectations can also have a profound impact on our perceptions. If you've grown up in a home where no one has ever gone to college, you may believe that you never will either. If you've applied for jobs and been rejected time and time again, you may come to believe that you will never get a good job. If you've never been asked out on a date, you may think that no one will ever ask you. You would be wrong on all counts.

Your perspectives, biases and expectations shape your perceptions of each of these events. Perception is an extremely powerful and important concept. Our reality is shaped by our perception. Our perspectives, our expectations and our biases shape our perception. By controlling our expectations, considering multiple perspectives, and by being aware of our biases, we can control our perception and see reality more clearly.

Leading a happy, successful and meaningful life requires that we not allow our biases, perspectives, expectations or perceptions to blind us. You need to try to see reality as clearly and objectively as possible, which means that you need to consider multiple perspectives.

CHAPTER FOURTEEN

The Power of Compassion

COMPASSION IS THE EMOTION that we feel in response to the suffering of others. The Golden Rule often embodies, by implication, the principle of compassion: "Do unto others as you would have them do unto you." Ranked as a great virtue in numerous philosophies, compassion is considered among the greatest of virtues.

The following excerpts from an article entitled "Compassion and the Individual" contain some thoughts of His Holiness, the fourteenth Dalai Lama of Tibet, on the meaning and importance of compassion:

> I believe that the purpose of life is to be happy. From the very core of our being, we simply desire contentment. From my own limited experience I have found that the greatest degree of inner tranquility comes from the development of love and compassion. The more we care for the happiness of others, the greater our own sense of well-being becomes. Cultivating a close, warm-hearted feeling for others ... is the ultimate source of success in life ... . The need for love lies at the very foundation of human existence. It results from the profound interdependence we all share with one another. When you recognize that all beings are equal in both their desire for happiness and their right to obtain it, you automatically feel empathy and closeness for them ... . Because we all share an identical need for love, it

131

is possible to feel that anybody we meet, in whatever circumstances, is a brother or sister. No matter how new the face or how different the dress and behavior, there is no significant division between us and other people. I believe that at every level of society—familial, tribal, national and international—the key to a happier and more successful world is the growth of compassion.

What is perhaps most remarkable about compassion is not just what it does for those who receive it, but what it does for those who practice it. Scientific studies indicate that people who practice compassion produce 100 percent more DHEA—a hormone that counteracts the aging process and also decreases the stress hormone cortisol. An experiment by Michael Norton, published in *Science*, shows that people tend to be happier when they give money to others than when they spend it on themselves. Elizabeth Dunn, in a recent study, also found a similar phenomenon in children as young as two years old.

Practicing compassion has been found to improve your health by strengthening your immune system, normalizing your blood pressure, lowering your stress and depression, improving your recovery from illness, and even extending your life. The true power of compassion is far greater than most of us can imagine. Practice compassion by doing something small each day to help others, even in a tiny way. Offer a smile or a kind word, do an errand or chore for someone in need, or just listen to another person talk about a problem. Try to do something positive for someone else. Try to ease someone's suffering.

Practice mindfulness while practicing compassion. Mindfulness means being present in the moment. It means being aware of and opening your heart to the suffering of others and appreciating the wonders of nature. Try to make compassion and mindfulness daily practices. Try to make them lifetime practices. The more compassionate you are and the more mindful and authentic you are, the more you and others will benefit.

Chapter Fifteen
Embrace Your Community, and It Will Embrace You

THE ORIGIN OF THE word "community" comes from the Latin word "communis," which means shared by all. So community literally means to share among each other. Communities are as varied as their members. Often people belong to multiple communities. Communities can be families, educational institutions, businesses, religious groups, or teams. Communities are the very essence of how we live and socialize with others. They provide a sense of identity and purpose, a sense of belonging.

While different communities have different roles in society, they all share similar characteristics. Communities provide members with a sense of belonging and purpose. Disadvantaged or marginalized people often have limited opportunities to develop any personal or professional communities. Their disadvantages (a physical or intellectual disability, a drug dependency or any other limiting characteristic) reduce their abilities to develop social networks.

Many gang members join gangs not because they want to live that life, but because they need the security and sense of belonging that a gang provides. The gang may even abuse them, but they stay because they think there is nowhere else to go.

Why Do We Need Communities?

We all need a sense of belonging. It doesn't matter how successful we are—if we have no one to share our successes with, life becomes meaningless. Love is impossible in isolation.

In our search for happiness and success, communities play a critical role. Relationships are essential to both our happiness and success. Communities are where we make friends, develop personal and business contacts, share experiences and resources, learn, teach, advise, and support one another. Communities provide us with networks of support. Whether you are a young person trying to find employment, a middle-aged person developing a new business or career, or an older person who needs companionship or care, it is through your participation in communities that you will be able to meet your individual needs. Understanding the importance of communities and actively participating in them is an important part of leading a happy, successful, and meaningful life.

Seek out organizations in your community that provide support. Virtually every community has groups and organizations whose mission is to help those within their community. If you're young, go on the Internet and search for youth support organizations in your community. Become part of your community. Gain what others in your community have to offer, and give back by showing pride and respect for the community you live in. Regardless of what community you live in, the people and resources in that community can add value to your life if you allow yourself to be open to them. Your community represents an incredible asset that can assist you and your family in achieving your goals. Embrace your community, and it will embrace you.

We also need to acknowledge and understand that America needs to do much more in this area. Not all communities are equal. While some offer a wide range of resources, others offer far less.

What Can We Learn From Other Communities?

We all belong to multiple public and private communities, some global, some national, and some local. We all also have roles to play in building, developing, and supporting each of those communities. There are many ways to do this. On a recent trip to Bali, an island province of Indonesia, certain features of the Balinese community impressed me. They are worth sharing and may offer insights into how you can help improve your community. They may even inspire you to action.

The first thing that impressed me relates to our global community. Indonesia is home to the world's largest Muslim population, with over 200 million Muslims. This represents about 13 percent of the world's Muslim population. Amid this predominantly Muslim population, sits the island of Bali, home to Indonesia's Hindu minority, which represents only 1.7 percent of the Indonesian population. The Balinese, who are overwhelmingly Hindu, represent an ethnic minority that is able to successfully coexist within a much larger Muslim community. This is possible because the two largest Muslim organizations in Indonesia, Muhammadiah and Nadhatul Ulama, preach tolerance toward Balinese Hinduism by referring to the *surah al-Kafirun* verse of *al-Quran*, "Your religion is your religion; my religion is my religion." This example of religious tolerance, shown by the vast majority of Indonesia's 200 million Muslims, stands in sharp contrast to the examples of religious intolerance shown by Muslim extremists like ISIS, but it is equally important and instructive.

It shows that one country, Indonesia, with the single largest Muslim population, practices religious tolerance, and it proves that groups like ISIS represent an extreme fringe of the Muslim community. That is not to say that Muslim extremism is not a danger. On the contrary, I view Muslim extremism as a grave danger—not simply because of the threat that it represents today but because of the threat that it has the potential to represent in the future. That being said, what Bali teaches us is the importance of drawing a bright, shining line between opposition to Muslim extremism and Muslims generally. The extremists are nothing like the majority of Muslims who act sensibly and compassionately. It is a serious mistake to conflate them. It also teaches us that we can learn something about religious tolerance from what may seem like an unlikely source, the Muslim community of Indonesia. Insights are everywhere if you're open to them.

Another feature of the Balinese community that impressed me was the training of its young hotel and service staff. An important strength of Indonesia's demographic composition, in relation to its economy, is that it has a young population. Indonesia's median age is 28.2 years old. It is vitally important that this young workforce has employment opportunities. The same need exists in most American communities. What I found in Bali that accounted for this highly trained and competent service staff was that Bali had numerous vocational training businesses. Virtually every young person that I spoke to who worked in Bali's tourist industry attended and graduated from one of these training facilities. We have a similar need for increased vocational training in America's communities. The answer is not more for-profit colleges that leave young people saddled with debt and offer few if any real and immediate employment opportunities. Instead, we need cost-effective, useful programs that focus on specific skill sets and result in meaningful employment with minimal debt.

The Balinese also impressed me with the sheer volume of their community gathering places. It made me realize how this important community resource is sadly lacking in American society. American society has many groups and civic organizations that provide resources and support, but we don't have an abundance of public areas for communities to gather spontaneously and independently for meetings, performances, learning opportunities, and social gatherings. In some but not all neighborhoods, we have parks, but we could be doing so much more. In Bali, Hindu temples stand on virtually every corner, and each of these temples has a public gathering space, where people can congregate and socialize even in the absence of religious services. These gathering spaces are not elaborate and expensive structures with restricted access. For the most part, they are simply covered, open-air spaces that provide a place for people of all ages to form community bonds. These spaces help to foster a sense of community and act as constant reminders of the importance of community.

When we consider how we could improve upon and elevate our neglected and impoverished communities, we should look to Bali's liberal use of community gathering spaces. America needs to invest in its neglected communities rather than allow them to further deteriorate into islands of discontent and breeding grounds of social unrest. One way to start would be to restrict the number of corner liquor stores and promote the development of community resources—parks, playgrounds, music venues, libraries, and simple open spaces where people can gather safely and connect with their communities.

We also need to understand that all U.S. communities are *our* communities. We can't afford to sit idly by, waiting for "the government" to improve them. That approach clearly isn't working, and when something isn't working, you need to pivot and try something different. I not only believe that we can improve our neglected communities, I believe that we must.

How can you improve your community? Work with your local representatives to pass or enforce existing ordinances that require landowners to maintain and improve their properties, or remove unsafe and dilapidated structures. Demand that your elected representatives regulate and restrict the number of liquor stores allowed in your community. Start a nonprofit. Find landowners who own some of the abandoned lots in your community. Ask them to donate one or more of their abandoned lots to your nonprofit for use as a new, beautiful public space. You may have to speak to or meet with dozens of landowners to find those who are willing to help, but you will eventually find some who share your vision of a better community and are willing to help. You may need to align yourself with an existing group or established members of your community to establish credibility, but you will eventually find people who share your vision of a better community and are willing to join you. Get landowners to donate their lot(s). If they have multiple properties, explain that an improved community will increase the value of their other properties. Once you secure a property, find contractors and craftsmen in your local community who are willing to donate their services to help improve that property. Organize local fund raisers to collect enough money to make simple improvements that build upon the efforts of your volunteers. Transform the donated properties from public blights to places where children can play and people of all ages can gather. Regardless of your social or political views, it is right to learn from these examples and to use them as inspirations to improve upon our own communities. It is in our common self-interest to create and restore safe, beautiful, and friendly community spaces in *all* of America's communities.

CHAPTER SIXTEEN

How to Deal with Authority

SOME HAVE OBSERVED THAT Millennials do not offer their respect to authority automatically. Instead, they expect others to act like their parents did and show them respect. This attitude can create a variety of problems when Millennials encounter employers, police, and other authority figures that don't share their views. Understanding the proper role of authority, the need for authority, and how to deal with authority are critically important for everyone. Clearly, understanding these issues is especially important for young people who may be inclined to question and/or challenge authority figures. In fact, having a clear understanding of these issues may make the difference between life and death.

Racism and Authority

In 2013, the hash tag #BlackLivesMatter was launched in response to the acquittal of George Zimmerman for the killing of Trayvon Martin. Since then, the killing of unarmed African-American men has continued unabated. While covering the riots that took place in Ferguson, Missouri, and Baltimore, Maryland, as a result of Michael Brown's and Freddie Gray's deaths, the media focused on racial tensions as the primary cause or catalyst for the riots.

Racism has existed for thousands of years, and despite the best efforts of many, it continues to be an intensely emotional and polarizing issue for millions of Americans. Racism is real. It is an intensely emotional and dehumanizing experience. It is offensive not only to its intended and unintended targets, but to all those whose senses of decency and morality abhor injustice. The idea that one man would judge another man inferior simply by the color of his skin is beyond ignorant. It is a cruel and intolerable assault on human dignity that no man or woman should be expected to endure.

A Lack of Respect for Authority

Lack of respect for police authority, primarily among the African-American community, is at levels not seen since the civil rights moment. In some American cities, distrust of the police and distrust of the judicial system are rooted in a long legacy of racism and injustice.

Before the abolition of slavery, police in the South would often be called upon to track down slaves. Later, they were involved in enforcing Jim Crow laws. During the civil rights struggles of the 1960s, police who were sworn to protect and serve entire communities frequently failed to defend the most vulnerable minority members of those communities. In some cases, police misconduct went well beyond a passive failure to defend and included active participation in racially motivated hate crimes and atrocities.

In many communities across this nation, people remember these appalling failures to protect and serve. Others have had more recent, direct, and personal experiences with the police and/or the judicial system that they considered demeaning, disrespectful, and demoralizing. Many minorities' views of police and the judicial system are influenced by these historical, personal, and life-changing experiences.

America has responded to racism with a variety of measures including, but not limited to the 13th, 14th, and 15th amendments to the U.S. Constitution; the 1954 U.S. Supreme Court decision of Brown v. Board of Education; the Civil Rights Act of 1964; the Voting Rights Act of 1965; and numerous state and federal rules and regulations designed to correct past wrongs.

While helpful and well intentioned, these legal responses have not eliminated and cannot eliminate racism in America. No legislation can. Racism is an attitude grounded in bias and perception. In many cases, these biases and perceptions have been handed down within families— generation after generation.

Understanding and Identifying Racism

Ending racism will require more than changes in law and social policy. It will require a fundamental shift in our individual biases and perceptions. Unfortunately, biases and perceptions often prove resistant to change.

Despite the best efforts of many, racism continues to undermine our national ethos and inflict pain and suffering on millions of Americans. These are complex, emotionally charged issues that have existed for generations. Only the continuing efforts and commitment of this and future generations can resolve these issues—and this will take time. Unfortunately, we may be running out of time.

Many young African-American men and women are out of work, and these numbers are only likely to increase. According to the latest information from the Bureau of Labor Statistics, the official unemployment rates for Americans (ages 16 to 19) are the following: whites, 15.7 percent; Hispanics, 20.8 percent; and African Americans, 31.8 percent. Note that the rate for young African Americans is double that for whites.

For many young men and women of color, attending college is not an option. Many of these young people have very few options. Some who lack employment opportunities simply loiter and engage in mischief, as young people of all races and backgrounds are inclined to do. In other cases, young men and women of color who are generally law abiding citizens may come into contact with police for minor traffic violations, such as speeding or expired license plates. Some young people who are unable to find work and lured by the lucrative underground economy turn to selling drugs or prostitution. Some get involved in more serious crimes. Many who are not engaged in any criminal activity are stopped by police simply because they live in neighborhoods with high crime rates, where police officers patrol more aggressively in an effort to deter and combat criminal activity.

Some advocates point to increased police activity in these neighborhoods, which disproportionately affects young African Americans, as examples of racism. They argue that African-American drivers are pulled over for minor traffic violations or stopped and searched far more often than Caucasians. Statistics support these claims.

Police respond to such claims by arguing that racial disparities in traffic enforcement and stop and frisks stem from the fact that more

African Americans live in high crime areas, where officers patrol more aggressively. Police argue that more vigilant police activity in these neighborhoods has nothing to do with racism and instead is simply good police work, designed to discourage increased criminal activity.

Claims of racial profiling, discriminatory enforcement, and racism are serious, complicated issues that require a case-by-case investigation and analysis. While it may be tempting for some to seize upon these statistical disparities in enforcement to support claims of police racism, such arguments have limited probative value. Numerous reasons other than racism could easily explain such disparities. By way of illustration, more men are stopped and frisked than women, and more young people are arrested than old people, yet no one would suggest that this provides evidence of gender or age discrimination. So why do some seize upon such statistical anomalies to support their claims of racism? In a word—bias.

Our biases shape our perceptions. While the biases of some police officers may shape their perceptions concerning who should be questioned, detained, or arrested, our own biases may similarly shape our perceptions about the motivations of police in questioning, detaining, or arresting us. In both cases, our biases in perception often mislead us.

Given the seriousness of the matter, claims of racism should, therefore, require a higher level of proof than mere statistical anomalies, and police officers' conduct should be judged on a case-by-case basis, just as we would expect our own actions to be judged.

To be clear, if police are, in fact, engaged in illegal and/or discriminatory enforcement, that would not only be indefensible—it would be actionable. While there is widespread agreement that such abuses do exist, it is likely that they do not exist to the degree that some whose own biases cloud their objectivity would like us to believe. This is a matter that requires further unbiased review and analysis. Are some police racist? Absolutely. Does this mean that large numbers of police officers are racist or that you should not trust or follow the instructions of police officers? Absolutely not!

Racism cannot be defeated through the application of bias any more than lies can be defeated with more lies. In the final analysis, racism is nothing more than a lie. It is a lie that some people cling to out of their own insecurity and impaired self-image. Much like drowning victims will pull down those around them to save themselves, racists attempt to reduce the stature of those whose skin color is different from their own in a misguided attempt to somehow elevate their own stature by comparison. Racists are fundamentally insecure, and they overcompensate for their insecurity by attempting to diminish others. Truth is the only means capable of ending racism, and truth requires objectivity. All people need to be treated equally, fairly, and objectively. Those who expect justice for themselves cannot deny it to others. It is, therefore, imperative that police officers be judged individually, honestly, and objectively, without bias or preconception, just as we expect our own actions to be judged.

Moreover, regardless of the reason for the encounter, when young people of all racial, ethnic, or socioeconomic backgrounds come into contact with police, whether or not the contact is justified or unjustified, whether or not the police officer has or has not shown bias, young people need to understand how to deal with that encounter intelligently, appropriately, and unemotionally. Their lives may depend on it.

I believe that those who seek to protect these young people by rushing to judgment, in pointing to racism as the primary cause for the increases we are seeing in police shootings or the primary cause for some of the statistical disparities that may exist in police enforcement, are wrong to do so. Here's why.

False Claims of Racism Promote, Rather Than Reduce Racism

To begin with, while racism is real, many claims of police racism are simply untrue. In many cases, claims of police racism are made well before any meaningful investigation, let alone any scientific or forensic examination, can occur. Rather than weigh the evidence calmly, objectively, and dispassionately, activists and media personalities, eager to strike a blow against racism, often rush to judgment.

The idea that most encounters between police officers and African Americans are racially motivated or influenced is an absurdity. Yet claims of racism are inevitably raised in most media-reported encounters between young African Americans and police. Moreover, while many are more than willing to hold police accountable for their actions, far fewer seem willing to hold those who are the subjects of such police actions accountable for their conduct. Videos that make the rounds on social media, some drawing national attention on mainstream media, are often edited to show only the altercation surrounding an arrest. Rarely, if ever, do they show what preceded the arrest, the full context of the arrest, or the illegal failure to comply that, in many cases, precipitated the arrest.

Some may even regard focusing exclusively on the conduct of the police, or the circulation of incomplete or edited versions of reality, as somehow justified or appropriate. Those with a strong bias against police may even welcome or encourage such distortion as a way to offset the relative disparity in power between disadvantaged youth and the police. Others may see every such encounter, regardless of the facts, as an opportunity to strike a blow against racism. The reality is that this approach, which has become all too common in the media, is neither justified nor appropriate. It is not only counterproductive to the goals of protecting young people and ending racism, it is extremely dangerous and can only serve to undermine both of these objectives.

Failures to hold all involved parties responsible for their actions and to present all facts and circumstances fully, fairly, and objectively have unintended and adverse consequences. The most significant of these is the erosion of respect for police authority.

Many young people who have been influenced by widespread claims of police racism are increasingly growing less likely to trust police officers and may fail to comply with lawful police orders or attempt to flee when approached by police officers. Others who are encouraged by ever increasing criticism of police may make false allegations of police racism to avoid the consequences of their own unlawful actions, gain leverage, generate publicity, make a political statement, or otherwise profit from their encounters with police.

In the long run, undermining the trust and confidence that young people have in police can only result in their being more likely to challenge police authority. This, in turn, can only result in more young people being arrested or, far worse, placed in life-threatening situations.

In Ferguson, Missouri, well before the Michael Brown shooting, young African Americans had lost all trust and confidence in police. The U.S. Justice Department reported that, between 2011 and 2013,

94 percent of the people arrested in Ferguson for "failure to comply" were African American. Over time, Ferguson's African-American youth simply stopped trusting or listening to police. Michael Brown, the 18-year-old African American who was shot and killed by Ferguson police officer Darren Wilson, was one of those youth. The police department in Ferguson, Missouri, has major issues that need to be addressed, not the least of which is the racial composition of the department. However, that is a separate and distinct issue from whether or not the shooting of Michael Brown was racially motivated. It was not.

If you read the March 4, 2015, "Department of Justice Report Regarding the Criminal Investigation into the Shooting Death of Michael Brown by Ferguson, Missouri, Police Officer Darren Wilson," you will be amazed to see how radically it differs from media accounts that fueled the Ferguson riots. I encourage everyone to read the report. Racism had absolutely nothing to do with this shooting. Media accounts were recklessly inaccurate.

Fueling an atmosphere of distrust for police is, in my opinion, an unwise and dangerous proposition. In addition to making conflicts between young African Americans and police more likely, it could also make young people less likely to seek the assistance of police—when such assistance could prove critical to their well-being or even lifesaving. In the end, the erosion of police authority benefits no one. It can only serve to make society less safe for all of us. In addition, for those who seek to reduce racism in America, using unsupported claims of police racism, based on supposition and conjecture and/or video chippings that have been edited to highlight confrontation, do nothing to reduce racism in America. They do just the opposite. They scream bias and undermine the credibility of those who rely upon them.

The only way to truly reduce racism in America is to change people's biases and perceptions. Claims of racism that are unsupported, inaccurate, or intellectually dishonest, however well intentioned, do not alter the biases and perceptions that lead to racism. They fuel and reinforce them.

We all need to be held accountable for our actions. Neither the color of our skin nor the color of our authority should insulate us from answering for our actions.

Most importantly, false claims of police racism send an inaccurate, dangerous, and irresponsible message to young people, and that message (that they should distrust police) may place them in even greater danger.

If and when racism is proved to have played a role in police shootings and/or police misconduct, it needs to be *exposed* and *vigorously prosecuted*. However, when police shootings and/or arrests of young African Americans are instantly and erroneously alleged to be examples of racism, such allegations undermine the credibility of those seeking to reduce racism in America and reduce their effectiveness.

In my opinion, more lives will be saved if we are less quick to judge and more objective and accurate in our analysis. Truth and truth alone needs to be our guiding principle. Not all young African Americans are guilty as charged, and not all are innocent. In order to reduce racism in America, we all need to join in an objective search for the truth and understand that it is in our common interest to hold all individuals accountable for their actions—regardless of race, ethnicity, age, gender, wealth, title, or position.

When Dr. Martin Luther King said, "I have a dream that one day my children will be judged, not by the color of their skin, but by the content of their character," he understood that we all are and should be judged by our characters. While it is critically important that individuals not be judged by the color of their skin, it is equally important that everyone, regardless of race, be held accountable for their actions and their characters.

Only by demanding universal adherence to both of these standards can there be any hope of reducing, let alone eliminating, racism in America. If we all want to live in a safe and civilized society, then respect for the rule of law cannot be optional. The decision to follow or not follow the lawful orders or instructions of a police officer cannot be based upon personal self-interest or circumstance. Compliance with the lawful orders of a police officer must be understood to be legally mandated and hence mandatory. Most important, compliance must be universal. You don't get a pass because you're rich or politically connected any more than you do because you're angry or a member of an oppressed minority armed with a cell phone camera.

The law requires that all of us obey the lawful orders of a police officer—period! Absent such understanding and agreement, this world will quickly devolve into chaos. When you look at these tragic police encounters, virtually all of them have one thing in common, and it is not race, geography, or economics.

In the vast majority of cases, tragic police encounters begin with a breakdown in communication. When police officers encounter someone who runs, someone who fails to follow their lawful orders, or someone with a defiant or disrespectful attitude, that encounter quickly results in failed communication and inevitably ends in escalation.

Generational differences relating to our varied perceptions about the proper role of police and authority are a common theme and a major contributing factor to the increases in police shootings we are all witnessing. Prior generations could generally be expected to respect authority. Rarely did they question or defy authority. That is not the case with Millennials. Far too often, Millennials of all ethnic backgrounds routinely question and defy authority. This is already raising serious issues between Millennials and police.

According to a study published by the *Journal of Pediatrics*, by the age of 23, up to 41 percent of young adults have been arrested at least once for something other than a minor traffic violation. *The Huffington Post* estimates the number of those arrested by age 23 to be as high as 50 percent of African-American males and 40 percent of Caucasian males.

This high arrest rate is troubling, not only because of the corrosive effects that system involvement and confinement can have on a young person's emotional, mental, and social development, but also because these arrest records will follow these individuals and make it far more difficult for them to get housing, obtain employment, loans, or an education. Regarding these high arrest rates, Eugene V. Beresin, a child psychiatrist at Massachusetts General Hospital and professor at Harvard Medical School, says, "Those are alarmingly high numbers. There are social, economic, educational, and family risks associated with arrests. And we all have to be concerned about that."

There are no doubt a number of reasons for these increases in arrests. But again, one of the major contributing factors may well be an increase in defiant attitudes and a lack of respect for authority. Police often exercise discretion in making arrests for minor infractions, and police officers are human beings. While some argue that such discretion is being exercised with racial bias, I would argue that a lack of respect for authority has a far greater influence on the exercise of police discretion than race. Common sense would suggest that police are less likely to arrest someone who is respectful than someone who is disrespectful, regardless of race. That's just human nature.

Changes in technology are also having an impact. Young people, armed with their cell phone cameras, now feel empowered to challenge, confront, and defy police. Activists eager to document police misconduct are encouraging young people to carry and use such devices to document their encounters with police. Society's obsession with fame is also having an influence. Want to get famous? Document an adverse encounter with police, post it on the Internet, and watch it go viral. Is this confrontational approach contributing to increased safety for young African Americans? Or is it contributing to an atmosphere of lawlessness that makes society less safe for everyone?

Focusing on sensitivity and communication training for police is clearly part of the solution. Yet, even this needs to be approached with caution. Police work is incredibly dangerous. These men and women perform an essential service in our communities, and that service does not include counseling or caretaking. It is ensuring our collective safety, which often requires that they take immediate and instinctive actions. In some cases, any hesitation can mean the difference between life and death.

Police work requires an authoritative presence. Their role is to provide a safe and secure environment for all citizens. In some instances, their adopting a less authoritative presence or tone may actually make them less effective and place them and the community they serve at greater risk of harm.

At what point will police officers, faced with angry and belligerent suspects, distracted by interlopers with cell phones, and surrounded by crowds gathering like storm clouds, say, "Enough! I'm not going into these neighborhoods anymore!" How safe will the law-abiding members of these communities be then?

A Failure of Communication between Police and Communities

Anyone who lives in crime-ridden communities would argue that police have already largely abandoned their neighborhoods. These communities have become overrun with violent gangs, criminals, and drug dealers. Police have very limited support in these communities. Most of the people who live in these communities are afraid to offer the police any assistance. They know that the police come and go while gangs are always present. This absence of community support increases the dangers police face in entering these neighborhoods and makes increased police presence less likely.

The hardworking, law-abiding citizens who live, work, and go to school in these crime-ridden neighborhoods are, therefore, forced to adapt to a life without police protection—a life where joining a gang or looking like a gang member increases, rather than reduces, their security. Survival in these communities is a completely different proposition from survival in the suburbs. Parents in high-crime neighborhoods send their children to get milk from the ubiquitous corner liquor store. Children often go to sleep with the sound of gunfire in the background. Young people in these communities don't see police as a reliable source of support and protection. They see them in a best-case scenario as irrelevant to their well-being and in a worst-case scenario as a threat to their well-being.

It is with this background that we need to examine the ongoing relationship between the young people who are living in these communities and the police whom we all rely upon to keep society safe.

The Need for Change

The reality is that there are no easy answers. These are complex problems that will require thoughtful and multidimensional solutions. Objectively analyzing and attempting to accurately assess and understand the true nature of these problems is simply a first step. Improving communication between community leaders and police must be part of the solution. Creating opportunities for increased cooperation between residents and police is another part of the solution. Reducing the threats of violence and intimidation within these communities is another part of the solution.

Hiring police who live in and are more reflective of the communities that they serve is part of the solution. Increasing understanding and empathy for the positions of all stakeholders, including police, is part of the solution. Fostering an environment that can attract investment, give rise to opportunity, and create jobs is part of the solution. Reducing the number of liquor stores permitted in these neighborhoods is part of the solution. Involving police in improving school safety and providing safe passage for children forced to walk through these communities is part of the solution. Redirecting police attention away from crimes like simple marijuana possession and graffiti is part of the solution. Creating community centers that take kids off the streets and provide a safe and secure environment for community gatherings is part of the solution. Teaching all young people to have greater respect for authority is an absolutely essential part of the solution.

"Failure to comply" is a major source of arrests in this country, and it shouldn't be. None of us, regardless of whether we are black or white, young or old, rich or poor, angry or calm, have the right to ignore or refuse to comply with the lawful orders of a police officer. Regardless of who you are, if you don't want to get arrested and if you want to be respected, you need to show respect to the men and women who put their lives on the line every day to protect and serve the society we all live in. This is true even if those police may be less visible, present, or revered in the communities you live in. Society has police to "protect and serve," but they are not our servants. They are ordinary men and women we rely upon to perform an extraordinary service. They risk their lives every day to ensure our safety and security. They deserve our respect.

Sergeant Henry Prendes

While serving as Nevada's attorney general, I had the honor of speaking at a memorial service honoring Sergeant Henry Prendes. Sergeant Prendes was shot and killed after responding to a domestic violence call involving a man beating a woman with a stick in the front yard of a home. Sergeant Prendes approached the door of the home when the suspect opened fire with a semiautomatic rifle, striking him. The suspect fired approximately 50 rounds and kept other officers pinned behind cars and walls. A member of the Las Vegas Metropolitan Police Gang

Unit heard the call and responded to the scene with a rifle. He was able to shoot and kill the suspect and help rescue Sergeant Prendes.

Sergeant Prendes died from the wounds he received that day. He had served with the Las Vegas Metropolitan Police Department for fourteen years. His wife and two young daughters survived him.

Think about these facts. Sergeant Henry Prendes died, leaving his wife and two young daughters without a husband and father, because he had the rare courage and conviction to place the safety of a woman he didn't even know above his own safety. If this is not a hero, I don't know what is.

This is what police officers do. They place themselves in harm's way to protect and serve us. They risk their lives for us. They die for us. They deserve much more than our respect. They deserve our gratitude and admiration.

Advice That May Save Your Life

Below are five pieces of advice that can keep you from getting arrested and may save your life. This is the same advice that I have given to my 18-year-old daughter and my 24-year-old nephew regarding how they should interact with police. It is surprisingly similar to the advice that Chris Rock offers, in his video "How Not To Get Your Ass Kicked By The Police." Check it out on YouTube, http://youtu.be/igQDvYOt_iA.

It doesn't matter if you are African American, Asian, Hispanic, or Caucasian. It doesn't matter if you are young or old, rich or poor, or if you are dealing with a good cop or a bad cop. It doesn't matter if you are in the right or in the wrong. My advice is the same regardless of circumstance.

It may be difficult for some who feel that they are being profiled, disrespected, or treated unfairly to follow this advice. Those who may have lost trust or confidence in the police, based on their views of the judicial system or the nature of their personal experiences, may find following my advice even more difficult. None of this makes the advice any less valid.

Police perform a necessary and dangerous job for society. On their initial contact with you, they have no way of knowing if you are or are not a threat to their personal safety. They cannot, should not, and will not take any unnecessary risks with their personal safety. You need to understand and accept that fact! And you need to resist the impulse, however well grounded, to respond emotionally. Any emotional, disrespectful, defiant, irrational, or even immature response during a police encounter increases the likelihood of an escalating police response—exponentially. Interacting with the police is not a matter that anyone should take lightly. It is not an opportunity for you to vent your frustrations or express your emotions. It is a serious encounter, filled with uncertainty and apprehension. The police are armed. The police are there for a reason. They may be investigating a possible crime. It could be a serious crime. They are empowered by law to investigate possible criminal activity. All citizens are legally required to comply with their lawful authority. The one group that is most likely to fail to comply is criminals. When you fail to comply, you are breaking the law. If you break the law, if you act like a criminal, you should reasonably expect to be treated like a criminal. If you don't want to be treated like a criminal, don't be one and don't act like one.

Regardless of the circumstances, you need to suppress and control your emotions. You need to comply with the lawful orders, commands, and instructions of all police officers, and you need to do so promptly and politely.

My five points of advice are as follow:

1. Don't break the law.

2. Show complete respect for the police at all times.

3. When interacting with the police, be open, honest, and forthright. Do not attempt to hide or conceal anything. Keep your hands out of your pockets and where they can see them. Do not make any sudden moves whatsoever.

4. Do *exactly* as you are told without delay and without objection. Never argue with a police officer. If you have an argument to make, you or your parents can make it with the district attorney, your lawyer, or the judge.

5. Do not involve yourself in police matters that do not involve you personally. Do not attempt to make arguments on behalf of someone else or in any way interfere with a police officer who is doing his or her job.

If you follow this advice, you will be far less likely to have any problem with 99 percent of the police officers you encounter. You will be less likely to be arrested, and you will come home to your family alive and well.

Parents—you should insist that your children follow this advice and provide an example to your children by following this advice yourselves.

If you choose to disregard this advice, understand that you do so at your peril. Police are human. They make mistakes. They have stressful jobs. They are constantly involved in high-risk encounters filled with uncertainty. They have families at home. They will protect themselves. They carry guns.

When you argue with a police officer or fail to immediately follow their lawful instructions, you create unnecessary risks for them, for yourself, and for others. *You make the situation far more dangerous for everyone. You have absolutely no right to do that!*

A civilized society cannot long endure if people are allowed, let alone encouraged, to challenge or interfere with police on the street. If you want to live in a civilized society, then you need to understand, accept, and embrace this concept. Failure to follow a lawful order of a police officer, interfering with a police officer, and resisting arrest are all crimes punishable by fines and/or imprisonment for good reason. Without these rules, all members of society would be at greater risk.

Do not attempt to substitute your judgment for theirs about what should or should not happen during an encounter with police. Accept and respect their authority. Do *not* disrespect them.

If you feel that you have an argument to make or you feel that your rights have been violated, *you are not without recourse.* Tell your parents, call a lawyer, or take it up with the judge. But *never* argue with a cop on the street! Anyone who advises you differently is giving you very bad advice and may be risking your life.

CHAPTER SEVENTEEN

The Company You Keep

L IFE IS ABOUT RELATIONSHIPS. In fact, nothing in life is more important. Love, family, and friendship are all about relationships. Some relationships enhance our life experiences. Others can harm us. We need relationships that enhance our lives. We need to avoid relationships that detract from our lives or harm us. Over the course of your life, you will meet many people. Some will become casual acquaintances. A select few will become friends.

The Meaning of Friendship

Friendship represents a unique class of relationship. Friends are not our family, yet we let them into our inner circle. They learn intimate details about us and have significant access to us. We trust them. Here are some wise words that have been said over the centuries about friendship:

+ Be slow to fall into friendship, but when thou art in, continue firm and constant.
  —Socrates, Greek philosopher

+ There is nothing on this earth more to be prized than true friendship.
  —Thomas Aquinas, Italian philosopher and theologian

+ Be courteous to all but intimate with few, and let those few be well tried before you give them your confidence.
  —George Washington, first American president

- A man's friendships are one of the best measures of
  his worth.
  —Charles Darwin, English naturalist and evolutionary
  theorist
- My best friend is the one who brings out the best in
  me.
  —Henry Ford, American industrialist
- Rare as is true love, true friendship is rarer.
  —Jean de La Fontaine, French poet

It takes time to determine whether the person you're spending time with is a true friend or not. Getting to know new people is an important part of life, but you need to surround yourself with the right people—people who add value, meaning, or purpose to your life rather than detract from it. You might really enjoy hanging out with a particular group on weekends, but who are these people? What do you really know about them?

Who Are Your Friends?

Friends come from all walks of life. They grow up in different places and different homes; they have different parents, different educations, different experiences; they are born with different mental and physical characteristics.

Best friends and high school sophomores Skylar Neese, Shelia Eddy, and Rachel Shoaf were inseparable. Living in Morgantown, West Virginia, the then-sixteen-year-olds were beautiful and sociable. They took selfies together. They spent time together. They were supposedly best friends forever (BFFs). Everything changed on July 6, 2012, when Neese's parents discovered she was missing. Shoaf later told authorities that she and Eddy had stabbed their best friend Neese to death. Why? They just stopped liking her. No other reason.

Clinical psychologist Martha Stout, former Harvard Medical School professor and author of *The Sociopath Next Door*, tells us that one in twenty-five Americans are sociopaths who simply do not feel shame, guilt, or remorse. Not all sociopaths are violent criminals; they may be your bosses, your ex-boyfriends/ex-girlfriends, or even your best friend.

Sociopaths are often charismatic. They use flattery, lies, and deception to lure you into their web of deceit. They prey upon your good nature and generosity for their own selfish purposes.

In 2012, Philip Dhanes died of alcohol poisoning at a Theta Chi hazing event at California State University, Fresno. Fifteen pledges had been placed in a room where they were told they had to drink eight bottles of hard liquor in order to leave.

In 2013, Chun "Michael" Deng died following a Pi Delta Psi hazing event at Baruch College in New York. He was blindfolded and wearing a backpack filled with sand. He fell over after being pushed, striking his head. Fraternity members delayed seeking medical attention for two hours. He died two days later. This case gained national attention, with multiple fraternity members facing numerous felony charges, including murder.

In 2014, Armando Villa was one of a group of Pi Kappa Phi pledges at California State University, Northridge. The pledges were left blind-folded on a hiking trail in Angeles National Forest in Los Angeles. Villa lost consciousness during the eighteen-mile hike out of the forest. He died from heat stroke.

These three young men all had one thing in common. They had some bad friends, friends who were not looking out for them, friends who did not place their interests ahead of their own, friends who were not there when they needed them.

One in five women who attend college in the United States are victims of sexual assault. The Hunting Ground, a documentary addressing this important issue, debuted at the 2015 Sundance Film Festival and later appeared on CNN. If you're a young woman in college or about to attend college, you need to watch this film. Parents and young men should watch it as well.

The people you select as "friends" and those you choose to associate with can have a profound impact on your life and safety. It is estimated that 25 percent of people (one in four) have some type of mental disorder. Some of these people may be people you call friends. Be careful. Look for warning signs. Stay away from people whom you have concerns about. If you sense danger, trust your instincts.

Personality Types You Should Avoid

The following Personality Inventory describes types of people who may appear to be your friends at first but who never make good friends. As soon as you realize someone you're associating with fits one or more of these types, avoid the person.

- *Takers.* Takers will use you for your assets, like your car, apartment, home, money, clothes, and friends.

- *Narcissists.* Narcissists are self-centered people who believe that life revolves around them. They don't care about you. They always find something to say or do to make themselves seem better than you.

- *Aggressive Personalities.* Aggressive personalities want to be better than you. They may attempt to get ahead by using your ideas and making themselves look good at your expense. Bullies also fit into this category. Even if they are not bullying you—avoid them.

- *Victims.* Victims always come to you with their problems. They are always going through hardships. But when you need advice or have a problem, they're not there for you.

- *Clingers.* Clingy friends can't share you with other people. When they see you with other people, they're jealous. Yet they are not above abandoning you when a "more important" person is around.

- *Fakes.* A fake friend smiles to your face, but when other people are around, they make you feel small. They may put you down verbally. They might promise to call you back but never do.

- *Gossips.* Gossips will try to learn more about you. They may want to get close to your network of friends. A person who gossips to you about others certainly gossips about you.

- *Elitists.* Elitists think it's all right to insult your heritage using derogatory slang words around you even when they know it offends you. This person doesn't accept you for who you are.

- *Crisis Addicts.* Crisis Addicts are always in crisis. They're always stressing you out. They create crisis. They're always late. They're always complaining.

- *Troublemakers.* Troublemakers love to cause chaos. They often take pleasure in creating problems for other people. This type of person will try to get you to cause trouble as well.

- *Critics.* Critics are people who constantly criticize your goals and ambitions. A true friend will only offer constructive criticism. A critic will constantly say something that you do or say is stupid or dumb.

- *Queens/Kings.* Queens and kings are dominating. They accept you only when you think or act like they do. They can be spiteful. If you challenge them, they might attempt to turn others against you.

Decide whether any people who fit these personality profiles are even worth keeping as acquaintances. If you have to associate with someone at work or school who's not really a friend, then keep a distance between yourself and this person. On the other hand, if this person has no important links to your life, you may wish to cut the bond entirely. It may be difficult to stay away from one of these people. If you feel intimidated or threatened by anyone, tell an authority figure, your parents, or someone you trust. Be alert.

Choose Your Friends Wisely

Ask yourself the questions appearing in Table 2, on pages 158-159, about the people you think of as friends to determine if they are true friends.

TABLE 2. Choosing true friends

Question	Yes	No
Do they fit into any of the categories of "personalities to avoid?"		
Would they visit you in the hospital?		
Would they come out and help you if you had a flat tire?		
Will they look out for your best interests and be there when you need them?		
Do they elevate your spirits?		
Do they truly listen to you?		
Are their comments about you to others positive?		
Will they let you know if they think you're making bad decisions?		
Do they encourage and support you?		
Do they help you grow and improve your overall well-being?		
Do they make time for you, not just text time, but real face-to-face time? Or do they just "like" your posts on Facebook?		
Do they push you to drink or encourage you to do other things that make you feel uncomfortable?		
Do they cause you to get into bad or difficult situations?		
Are they a positive or a negative influence on you and your behavior?		
Could you turn to them in a crisis?		
Do you have doubts about whether or not you can count on them?		
Do they often come up with excuses for not being there when you need them?		
Will they keep your secrets?		
Do they love you the way you are?		
Are you always the one who has to initiate contact, or do they call you as well?		

Source: Created by author.

TABLE 2. Choosing true friends (cont'd)

Question	Yes	No
Do you always have to go see them, or do they come to see you as well?		
Are they someone your other friends like?		
Does your family like them?		
Do they have jobs?		
Would your employer hire them?		
Would you want your employer to meet them?		
Are they honest with you and others?		
Do they show compassion for others?		
Are they punctual when meeting you?		
Do they offer to cover their share of joint expenses?		
Do you feel as if you're being used?		
Do they have good character?		

Source: Created by author.

True friends are a treasure. When you have good friends, life can be a lot easier. Friendships bring you laughter, joy, tears, advice, companionship, and compassion. True friends are there for you through the good times and the bad times.

Many so-called friendships are not healthy; in fact, many people are bad friends. If you have a bad friend, then the best thing to do is to end the relationship. Bad friends can be mentally and emotionally draining. They can hold you back, or worse, as Skylar Neese discovered. You don't need to confront them; just back away. Start to limit your contact with them until you no longer have any contact. Again, *if you sense any risk at all, trust your instincts—tell your parents or an authority figure about these people.* Choose your friends wisely, and be a good friend. Ask yourself how your friends would rate you on the Personality Inventory. We all exhibit some of these poor traits occasionally. We may have moments when we are selfish or thoughtless. No one is a perfect friend 100 percent of the time, but we should all try to be great friends.

If you feel you are exhibiting some of the negative personality traits described in the Personality Inventory on pages 156-157, perhaps you need to do more to be a good friend. I know I have work to do in this area. I don't reach out to my friends as often as I should. I need to reach out more often. "The only way to have a friend is to be one" (Ralph Waldo Emerson, American essayist, lecturer, and poet).

Relationships, both positive and negative, can have a huge influence on your life. Your friends can influence virtually every choice you make. They can be a source of inspiration or a source of discontent and even depression. They can encourage you to succeed or enable you to fail. They can help you develop courage or undermine your self-confidence. They can be like a sail that moves you forward or an anchor that holds you back. The individuals you choose to surround yourself with will profoundly impact your life. Choose your relationships wisely!

CHAPTER EIGHTEEN
The Perils of Consumerism

COMPANIES MAKE MONEY BY selling us their goods and services. The more they can entice us to spend, the more profits they make. The mechanisms utilized to entice us to spend are advertising and marketing campaigns. Companies have become incredibly good at designing and deploying these devices. They spend billions to perfect and billions more each year to pursue their advertising and marketing strategies.

Psychologist Susan Linn of Harvard Medical School in her book, *Consuming Kids*, says, "Comparing the marketing of today with the marketing of yesteryear is like comparing a BB gun to a smart bomb; it's enhanced by technology, honed by child psychologists and brought to us by billions of dollars."

You Have a Target on Your Back

You need to understand that you have been the target of corporate advertising and marketing since before you were born. It has continued, unabated, every day of your life. You cannot help but be influenced by it. What is important is that you try to be aware of it. You cannot possibly be aware of all of the attempts to influence and control your behavior.

Much of today's advertising is subliminal. It targets the unconscious parts of your brain that function outside of your awareness. In a wine study, four French and four German wines, matched for price and dryness, were placed on the shelves of a supermarket in England. French and German music were played on alternate days above the display. On days when the French music played, 77 percent of the wine purchased was French. On days when the German music played, 73 percent of the wine purchased was German. Clearly, the music influenced consumers' purchases, but when asked whether the music influenced their choices, only one shopper in seven said it had. What is equally important is that you appreciate the influences that advertising and marketing have not only on you, but also on everyone around you.

According to *Direct Marketing* magazine, by the age of eight, children now make most of their own buying decisions. Advertising aimed at children is ubiquitous. Every avenue of children's play and entertainment is branded. By the age of seventeen, teenagers all over the world will have been exposed to hundreds of thousands of advertisements. In many cases, the influence of advertising on children is greater than the influence of their parents, their siblings or their peers.

The consumer world that children are immersed in is also extremely addictive. Child psychologist Allen D. Kanner, coeditor with Tim Kasser of the book *Psychology and Consumer Culture: The Struggle for a Good Life in a Materialistic World*, says, "Teens are inundated with so much marketing about the importance of brands to identity and image, it has changed the way they socialize with each other, interact with adults and view themselves and the world."

The culture of consumerism created by these relentlessly targeted campaigns affects all of us to a degree that is difficult to comprehend. We are all persuaded that we will not be happy unless we have the toys, games, clothes, iPhones, computers, cars, houses, food, and drinks that other people think are cool. What is most disturbing is that this insidious message, which we have grown up with our entire lives, is simply not true.

Possessions Can't Bring You True Happiness

Happiness has nothing to do with material possessions. Our happiness is not determined by how many Chanel handbags, Rolex watches, cars, boats, or houses we possess. The world is filled with millions of unhappy people who have all of these things and much more. While money may be able to contribute to your happiness, by allowing you to pay bills or take trips to relieve stress, material possessions can't bring you true happiness. Yet, many of us believe that they can.

We go through life spending money that we haven't yet earned to buy things that we don't really need to impress people that we don't care about. Why? Because we have been programmed by the millions of advertising and marketing messages we receive over our lifetimes to believe that consumerism is our path to happiness. Advertising and marketing are effective. They work. That's why companies spend billions of dollars on them. Advertisements are designed to penetrate our psyches. They influence our thoughts, feelings and behaviors.

What we have all been programmed to believe is simply not reality. It's a lie. It is a lie that is particularly difficult to recognize when we are young, because when we are young, our responsibilities are at their lowest point in our lives. We don't have to worry about supporting ourselves, about raising a family, about paying for our children's education, about rising health care costs, or retirement. All of these things seem like distant obligations when we are young. They seemingly don't apply to us. During this period of relative irresponsibility, we derive the most joy from our toys, but this doesn't last.

Don't misunderstand. I love my iPhone. I enjoy a great bottle of wine. I still buy clothes I don't need—and I get a certain sense of joy from most of the things I purchase. However, at some point, further consumption becomes pointless. More importantly, it can harm us. How many suits does a man need? How many pairs of shoes does a woman need? How big does anyone's house need to be?

As we get older, we begin to realize that we can't take our toys with us. We begin to understand that our gadgets won't pay the rent. They won't put food on the table. They won't help us provide for those we love. They won't allow us to retire and maintain our dignity and independence. They won't allow us to travel and see the world. Only when we begin to focus on our broader, more long-term needs, do we begin to recognize how truly unimportant our material possessions really are.

At Ignition 2014, a conference sponsored by a business website (businessinsider.com), Mark Cuban, serial entrepreneur and owner of the Dallas Mavericks, was asked what advice he would give to a 20-year-old. His answer was, "Don't use credit cards. Stay away from credit."

Berkshire Hathaway CEO and Chairman Warren Buffett spoke about Coca-Cola and how after dividends, stock splits, and patient reinvestment, someone who bought just $40 worth of Coca-Cola's stock when it went public in 1919, would now have more than $5 million—today that number is actually more than $10 million.

Yes, $40 in 1919 was very different from $40 today. However, even after factoring for inflation, it turns out to be $540 in today's money. Put another way, would you rather buy an Xbox One or invest the cost of an Xbox One in a stock that could one day be worth millions? The next time you're thinking of buying an iPhone, you may want to think about the long-term benefits of buying shares of Apple stock instead. Beware of the false promises of consumerism. Think and plan ahead.

CHAPTER NINETEEN

Luck Travels in the Sphere of Efficiency

A DEAR FRIEND AND former client of mine is a man named Abelardo Rodriguez. His father was General Abelardo Rodriguez, a former president of Mexico. Abelardo is 96 years old and still going strong. We were out golfing one day at his country club in La Jolla, California. He was approximately 80 years old at the time and still a great golfer. He hit an errant shot off the tee on a par three. The ball took a lucky bounce and landed on the green. I remember saying, "Lucky bounce." He smiled and said, "There's an old Mexican saying; the translation is "Luck travels in the sphere of efficiency." He was right.

Professional golfer Gary Player once said, "The more golf balls I hit, the luckier I get." Yes, there is pure chance. Pure chance can sometimes yield good luck or bad luck. Timing is another important factor that can alter outcomes, so much so that some even say, "Timing is everything." It can be, but have you ever noticed that successful people also seem to be unusually lucky? Their timing often seems impeccable. Here's why.

We Make Our Own Luck

Richard Wiseman, a psychologist from the University of Hertfordshire, UK, and author of The Luck Factor, found that those who call themselves lucky score higher on the personality factor of extroversion. That means that they are more likely to have a lucky encounter because they meet lots of new people and keep in touch with a large group of friends and acquaintances. Today there's a newer name for this. It's called networking.

165

Millennials are great at networking. Tools like Facebook, LinkedIn, Twitter, Instagram, and Snapchat have taken networking to new levels. Extroverts also score higher in personality tests on openness and lower in neuroticism, the tendency to experience negative emotional states like anxiety, anger, guilt, and depression.

Wiseman conducted an experiment in which he placed the same two chance opportunities, 1) money on the ground and 2) a potential encounter with a connected businessman in the paths of two different people. One claimed she considered herself an unlucky person; the other said he considered himself lucky. The "lucky" guy immediately noticed the money on the ground and pocketed it. He also struck up a conversation with the businessman in the coffee shop where the businessman had been planted. The "unlucky" woman stepped right over the cash. She sipped her coffee and left without saying anything to the same businessman.

Chance favors people who have a more open approach to life. An open person heads to the gym thinking he might encounter a potential new friend, business contact, or romantic interest. A closed person sees only other people working out.

Be Open and Flexible

You need to remain flexible to become aware of hidden opportunities. Open and flexible people are more fearless about trying something new. Increase your opportunities for good luck by maintaining a large network of friends and acquaintances. Stay connected.

Mental flexibility should also be cultivated. Think about different points of view when considering any topic. Perhaps you have a firm belief about the decision of the grand jury in Ferguson, Missouri, or about immigration, gun control, global warming, or gay marriage. If that's the case, regardless of your position, try to come up with reasons why your position might actually be wrong. It doesn't matter if you're for or against any given topic. Train your mind to see both sides of every issue. By doing so, you're training yourself to be open to new ideas. Openness is critical to learning and to luck.

Mix up your daily routine. Take varied routes to work, try stopping at out-of-the-way places for a cup of coffee. Try new lunch or dinner spots. Try to get out more often. Frequenting new places increases your chances of making new connections and discovering new opportunities.

Have a Positive Attitude

Try to keep your mood positive in order to be receptive to the possibilities presented to each of us every day. Researchers at the University of Toronto demonstrated the benefit of a positive attitude. They found that people in good moods take in more visual information, while those in bad moods don't see as much around them. Anxiety gives us tunnel vision. We end up missing potentially beneficial information.

Listen to your intuition. If you're truly unsure about a decision, ask yourself, "What's the worst that can happen? What's the true likelihood of that negative outcome?" says Wiseman. Whether or not any chance you take turns out well or badly, you will eventually benefit greatly from regularly seizing opportunities. For the most part, we make our own luck. Be open, be positive, and be flexible. You'll get lucky more often.

Chapter Twenty

Respect Your Elders

Ancient cultures in India, Europe, Asia, Africa, and Latin America all have long traditions of elder respect. The older citizens of ancient Greece and Rome were highly respected for their wisdom. Councils of elders helped rule Greek and Roman society. In Greek and Greek-American culture, old age is still honored and celebrated. The same is true of Italian families. Respect for elders is central to Greek and Italian families. I grew up in one of those Greek-American families.

The traditional basis for elder respect in Asian cultures is Confucian teachings. In the teachings of Confucius, respect for elders is a central theme. Filial piety (respect for one's parents, elders, and ancestors) is seen as an essential foundation for a good society. Essentially, these teachings direct offspring to recognize the care and aid received from their parents and, in return, to show respect to their parents.

Material support for one's parents is not all that is expected. Deference to your elders and a genuine inner reverence for them is expected as well. According to Confucius, elder respect must also extend beyond the boundary of the family. "At home, a young man should be dutiful towards his parents; going outside, he should be respectful towards other elders and be cautious in deeds and trustworthy in words" (*Analects of Confucius* [Lun Yu], 1996, Book 1, Chap. 6).

The teachings of Confucius require providing care and services for elders, serving them foods and drinks of their choice, bestowing gifts on them, using respectful language in speaking to and addressing them, having a courteous appearance when greeting them, furnishing them with honorable seats or places at gatherings, celebrating their birthdays and anniversaries, respecting all elders in society, being obedient, holding funeral rites for deceased parents, and revering ancestors.

These are beautiful teachings. Confucius could not have been more right. These teachings are essential to the foundation of any great society. Growing old is difficult. Anything that can make the transition into the final phase of one's life easier is a true blessing and a wise foundation for any society.

We all grow old. Whenever you look at an elderly person, understand that one day that will be you! The Golden Rule says, "Do unto others as you would have them do unto you." Think about that when you interact with your elders. Treat your elders as you want to be treated when you're old, and teach your children to do the same. Respect is something you have to give in order to receive it.

Why You Should Respect Your Elders

When you were young, unable to walk, talk, or feed yourself, your parents cared for your every need. They fed you. They washed you. They carried you. They clothed you. They sheltered you. They loved you. They stayed up all night worrying about you. You couldn't have survived without them.

Now that they are old, they need you. They may have vision problems, they may have trouble walking, and they may be unable to wash or feed themselves. Are you going to abandon them in their time of need? Is that what you want your children to do to you?

Elders represent an amazing knowledge bank. Why wouldn't we ask their advice or strongly consider giving deference to their opinions? Simply by virtue of their age, your elders have seen more than you have. They may not know what you know. Their experiences may be very different from yours, but that does not mean that you can't learn from them. On the contrary, you can learn a great deal from them.

Someone who has lived a long life has a different perspective from someone who is seeing things for the first time. With this experience comes wisdom that can be handed down. Your elders know you better than anyone and are, therefore, in a better position to advise you than most. Ask their advice. Learn from them.

Even the Bible addresses this issue directly in Proverbs 19:20, "Listen to advice and accept instruction, that you may gain wisdom in the future."

Your elders love you. They want what's best for you. They have seen you grow up. They have been there for you throughout your life. We are products of our past. Who we are derives in large part from our parents and our ancestors. Disrespecting those who came before us is essentially disrespecting ourselves.

How to Show Proper Respect

Address all elders with courtesy and respect. Call them Mom or Dad if they're your parents—they've earned that title. Never call them by their first names unless they have specifically asked you to do so. It's disrespectful. It doesn't make you look older. It makes you look immature and disrespectful.

If older people are not members of your family, address them as Mr. or Ms., followed by their last name. If they want you to call them by their first name, they will tell you. Honor their request. When approaching or greeting your elders, always make eye contact, smile, and shake their hand. A warm smile from you can brighten anyone's day.

Offer assistance. When an elderly person approaches an entrance to a building, hold the door and allow him or her to go first. Offer to reach for something on a high or low shelf in a store or at home.

Give them some of your time and attention. Most people who are older than you will appreciate having any amount of your attention. Sit down with a grandparent or another elderly person and show them that you care. Play a board game with them or watch a movie together. Ask questions about their experiences and then listen to what they have to say. If the elderly person is a grandparent, aunt, uncle, or other family member, show them that you love them. Offer a hug and say something affectionate. Ask questions about your family history.

Show good manners. Most of your elders were taught proper etiquette when they were children. Always say, "Please" and "Thank you." Let them know that you have good manners and good character traits. They will feel proud of you. They will know that they had something to do with it. Treat your elders as you want your children to treat you. Lead by example.

CHAPTER TWENTY-ONE

Managing Your Money

YOU'RE MAKING MONEY FOR the first time in your life, and you're also paying your own rent, bills, and student loan debts. This may be the first time you're on your own. You want to have fun. You want to enjoy the rewards of your hard work. You want to go out with your friends, go to concerts, travel.

You may have thought about saving, but you don't know how you're going to do it. There are so many things you want. You try to stop spending money, but it's difficult. Other people buy things like iPhones and designer clothes, so why can't you? You feel the need to keep up with your peers, whose successes and acquisitions are plastered all over Facebook and Instagram.

Saving money is difficult to justify. It takes too long to see any meaningful results. Retirement is not a priority for you. It may not even be a thought.

Senator Elizabeth Warren (D-MA) wrote a book with her daughter, Amelia Warren Tyagi, called *All Your Worth: The Ultimate Lifetime Money Plan*. Their rule of thumb is 50/30/20. Fifty percent of your take-home pay should go to your needs, 30 percent to your wants, and 20 percent to savings. This is great advice.

Most professional financial planners will tell you to take advantage of your workplace's 401(k) plan—if one is offered. This is also great advice. Always put enough money in to at least get the company to match your contribution. The average match is usually in the 3 to 4 percent range. Ignoring the matching contribution is like turning down a 3 to 4 percent raise every year. This is a painless way to start building a retirement savings balance. Roth IRAs are also a good way to save money and minimize taxes.

To make sure you understand the importance of saving early and often, consider the following example. If you invest $200 a month beginning at age 25, and you earn 7 percent annually on that money, by the time you turn 65, you will have about $525,000 saved. If you wait until you're 35 to begin saving, you'll have amassed less than half that amount—about $244,000. This shows the impact of compounding interest.

Some professional financial planners will argue that young people are in the perfect position to take on risk. Their logic is that young people can buy stocks and allow the markets and compound interest to work for them in the many decades they have to allow their money to grow.

The stock market is great for people who know what they're doing. The problem is that most people who invest in the stock market don't know what they're doing, and they are competing against professionals who know much more. Buying mutual funds, where your risk is spread over multiple stocks, may be a great idea. Buying individual stocks is a different proposition. When you buy a stock, someone who thinks he knows more than you do is selling that stock. Unless you know more than most or can devote hours to studying stocks, the market has significant risks.

While it is true that you can better afford to take risks when you are young because you have more time to recover from your mistakes, that does not mean you should play the market. Depending on the timing of your entry into the stock market and the timing of your exit, the results can vary widely, resulting in significant losses or gains. There's an old saying that "timing is everything." Therefore, most people who counsel you to invest in stocks will recommend that you buy and hold stocks in established companies and hold them over the long term.

Personally, I invest very little in the public stock markets. My cousin, legendary short seller James S. Chanos, is heavily involved in the stock market. He loves it. Many of his trades, like being the first to recognize that Enron was a house of cards, have gained national attention. He also predicted the 2008 housing crisis years before it happened and was one of the first to warn of major instability in China's economy. He has been consistently successful in researching, identifying, and evaluating significant opportunities in the stock market for over thirty years. He's brilliant, and he studies the markets and the stocks he trades relentlessly. Understand that while you may be investing in a high-flying stock, others who have far more information than you do may be shorting the very same stock. Over time, you may want to give the question of investing in the stock market further thought. It's an important decision. Read and learn more about investing in the stock market, and determine what level of involvement, if any, makes sense for you.

Many financial advisors will tell you that you should save from three to six months of your expenses for emergencies. If that is too difficult, consider putting aside $1,000 or more in a savings account for unforeseen expenses. Consider online savings accounts, which offer higher interest rates than brick-and-mortar banks.

Avoid debt. If you have debt—pay it off. You should be laser focused on getting rid of any student loans or credit card debt. Debt is your enemy. Don't get comfortable holding on to debt. If you have outstanding debts, consider paying off the smallest balances first. It's important to establish the behavior of both saving and debt reduction.

Have a plan in place for any extra money you make, like bonuses, tax refunds, annual raises, or side income. Consider using one-third of the extra money for things you want, one-third for debt repayment or replenishing emergency savings, and one-third for longer-term savings, such as retirement.

Buying a bigger car and moving into a more expensive apartment are normally very bad choices when you are just starting out. Those aren't just short-term spending decisions; those are long-term commitments that permanently commit you to higher spending in the future.

Invest in yourself. Invest in your "human capital" and future earning potential. Investing $2,000 in yourself on classes that improve your job skills and get you a $1,000 raise can, over time, be one of the wisest investments you can make. Anything that actually increases your earning potential is a good investment. But the investment you make really needs to improve your earning potential. Some for-profit schools do just the opposite. They saddle you with crushing debt while doing little if anything to increase your true earning potential. Make sure that any investment you make in education is with a reputable institution that can truly improve your earning potential in a meaningful way.

CHAPTER TWENTY-TWO

Finding Happiness

S INCE 1972, ACCORDING TO surveys funded by the National Science Foundation, only about one-third of Americans have described themselves as "very happy." Since 2004, the share of Americans who identify themselves as optimists has dropped from 79 percent to 50 percent. More than 20 percent of us will suffer from a mood disorder at some point in our lifetimes, and more than 30 percent from an anxiety disorder.

What Do We Know about Happiness?

According to Nancy Segal, a psychologist at California State University, Fullerton, and author of *Born Together—Reared Apart*, there is some evidence that genetics plays a role in happiness. Exactly what role and how much of a role are matters of opinion. Segal believes the role of genetics is substantial. Others consider the role of genetics to be less significant.

The Harvard Study of Adult Development, which began in 1937, is one of the most comprehensive studies of mental and physical well-being ever conducted. Research led by Dr. George Vaillant followed the lives of 268 Harvard sophomores for seventy-two years. Vaillant identified seven major factors that predict healthy aging, both physically and psychologically. The seven major factors that Vaillant found to be significant in determining our health and happiness were *employing mature adaptations, education, a stable marriage, not smoking, not abusing alcohol, exercise, and a healthy weight.*

Of the 106 men who had five or six of these factors in their favor at age 50, half of them (by age 80) were what Vaillant called "happy-well," and only 7.5 percent ended up as "sad-sick." Of those who had three or fewer of these factors at age 50, none ended up "happy-well" at 80. Also, those with three or fewer of these factors at 50, were three times as likely to be dead at 80, than those who had four or more of these factors in their favor.

Employing mature adaptations was considered one of the most important of the seven factors. Vaillant concluded that the way we "adapt" to our circumstances played a major role in our physical and mental health and happiness. He said:

> Much of what is labeled mental illness simply reflects our unwise deployment of defense mechanisms. Such mechanisms are analogous to the involuntary grace by which an oyster, coping with an irritating grain of sand, creates a pearl. Humans, when confronted with irritants, engage in unconscious but often creative behavior.

To deal with the circumstances we encounter, we adapt. How we adapt has a major influence on our health and well-being. The unhealthiest adaptations include paranoia, hallucination, or megalomania. One level up are unhealthy adaptations involving uncontrolled behaviors and imaginings, such as acting out, passive aggression, hypochondria, projection, and fantasy. The healthiest or mature adaptations include altruism, humor, anticipation (looking ahead and planning for future discomfort), and sublimation (finding outlets for potentially harmful feelings, like channeling aggression into sports; or potentially distracting feelings, like channeling fantasies into writing).

Vaillant also found that relationships played a critical role in a healthy and happy life. "It is social aptitude," he wrote, "not intellectual brilliance or parental social class, that leads to successful aging." When asked what he had learned from the study, Vaillant said, "*The only thing that really matters in life are your relationships to other people.*"

What Factors Contribute to Happiness?

Money. Numerous studies have found that money can make people happier insofar as it relieves pressure from everyday life. A study led by psychologist Edward Diener of the University of Illinois, analyzed the responses of 806,526 people in 135 countries collected over the course of six years. It found that income corresponds more or less directly to happiness but only if a person's wealth and aspirations keep pace. "Money can boost happiness if it allows people to obtain more of the things they need and desire," says Diener. "But when their desires outpace what they can afford, even rising income can be accompanied by falling feelings of well-being."

Although the true effect of money on happiness may be the subject of some debate, there is universal agreement that unemployment and poverty clearly lead to unhappiness, often resulting in divorce, depression, disease, and even suicide.

Work. Many believe that work is essential to happiness. Franklin D. Roosevelt (32nd U.S. president) said, "Happiness lies not in the mere possession of money; it lies in the joy of achievement, in the thrill of creative effort."

Optimism. In his book Learned Optimism, Martin E. P. Seligman points out that optimism lessens stress and increases longevity. He says, "Optimists are unfazed by defeat. Confronted by a bad situation, they perceive it as a challenge and try harder." According to studies published by *The Journal of Positive Psychology,* just trying to be happy can boost your emotional well-being. Those who actively tried to feel happier in the studies reported the highest level of positive moods.

Giving. Studies have shown that people who volunteer and do things for others are generally happier and experience better physical health and less depression. A study published in the journal *Science* found that spending money on other people has a more direct impact on one's happiness than spending money on oneself.

Exercise. Exercise has been shown to ease symptoms of depression, anxiety, and stress, thanks to the various brain chemicals that are released that amplify feelings of happiness and relaxation.

Laughter. A 2010 study that focused on the effects of laughter on the body concluded, "The body's response to repetitive laughter is similar to the effect of repetitive exercise." The study found that some of the benefits associated with working out, like a healthy immune system, controlled appetite, and improved cholesterol can also be achieved through laughter.

Music. Music has also been linked to happiness. Over a three-month period, researchers from the Group Health Research Institute found that patients who simply listened to music had the same decreased anxiety symptoms as those who had hour-long massages.

Relationships. A study published in *Psychological Science* found that those who take part in more substantive conversations and less trivial chitchat experienced more feelings of satisfaction. Spending real, meaningful time interacting with the people you care about (not texting and tweeting) is important to increasing your sense of well-being. "There's a deep need to have a sense of belonging that comes from having personal interactions with friends," says John Cacioppo, the director of the Center of Cognitive and Social Neuroscience at the University of Chicago. While social media keeps us in touch on a superficial level, truly loving, responsive interactions can only take place in person.

Spiritual/Religious Practice. Studies point to a link between religious and spiritual practice and happiness. As Ellen L. Idler writes in *The Psychological and Physical Benefits of Spiritual/Religious Practices,* "Transcendent spiritual and religious experiences have a positive, healing, restorative effect, especially if they are built in to one's daily life." Spiritual and religious practice can be a very important part of people's lives. To some people, it is the most important part of their lives. This as a very personal and individual choice. If this is something that is important to you, there are many spiritual and religious resources that are available to you in virtually every community.

Choice. According to Remez Sasson, founder of Success Consciousness, happiness lies within each of us. We tend to associate it with external events, possessions, and people. Sasson believes it actually has more to do with our thoughts than with external realities. He argues that happiness is about attitude and choice. "Happiness is always with us," he says, "but like clouds that block the sun, our happiness is blocked by our thoughts, desires and fears." Sasson says that we need to choose to be happy. We need to relax our minds and look within to experience happiness. He links past happiness as a way to affect current actions: Think about how you felt when you had a success—even when you were a child—and then visualize that event and feel those same feelings. Think about what you want to achieve now, and place your current goal together with those earlier happy feelings. Sasson says, "... thoughts charged with emotion materialize faster."

Mindfulness. Susan Albers, a psychologist at the Cleveland Clinic, holds a similar view, suggesting that we use mindfulness techniques to achieve feelings of happiness. Mindfulness means being present and in the moment and observing in a nonjudgmental way. Mindfulness comes from Buddhism and is key to meditation in that tradition. Stop and smell the roses. Look up at the sky on a bright, sunny day and marvel at the passing clouds. When you eat something wonderful, smell it, touch it, savor it, stop and think about each bite that you take. Be mindful of your daily activities and the beauty in nature that surrounds you.

Health. Happiness is also tied to health. Longevity guru Dean Ornish, founder of the Preventive Medicine Research Institute in San Francisco, points to four decades of research that support a simple prescription for improved health: "Eat well, move more, stress less, and love more."

In sum, happiness comes from a variety of sources in our lives, and we all have the power to control and increase our levels of happiness in many ways. Attitude is important. Relationships and compassion are important. Adaptation—how you deal with life's challenges—is extremely important. You need to be realistic. Adjust your needs, expectations, and wishes to fit reality. Exercise, laughter, and enjoying life's simple pleasures, like listening to music and taking time to be with good friends, are essential. Meditation, mindfulness, and spirituality enhance our appreciation of each day. To be happy, we must first look within ourselves and make conscious choices. Choose to be happy!

Conclusion

SIMPLY BY INVESTING THE time required to read this book, you have moved your life forward toward achieving a happy, successful, and meaningful life. You've gained important knowledge and insights that you can now use to advance your objectives. Leading a happier, more successful, and more meaningful life begins with your choosing that life for yourself. Anything is possible if you believe in yourself and do what's required to achieve your goals. Success doesn't just happen. It requires determination, commitment, and hard work. Most importantly, it requires that you make good choices.

The fact that you would take the time to read this book says a number of things about you. It says that you want more out of life. It shows that you have a desire to learn and improve your condition. It indicates that you have intellectual curiosity and the capacity to achieve. It confirms that you are capable of making good choices. It proves that you are willing to take action.

You have already taken an important first step in preparing for the journey that lies ahead. Your choices and your actions from this point forward will shape and determine your destiny. Summon the courage and commitment to achieve your goals, and continue moving forward with determination and a sense of urgency. Exercise control over your thoughts and your fears. Plan your next steps and then execute on that plan. Think before you act. Let your strength of character and your infectious, optimistic attitude speak more loudly than anything you could say. Communicate honestly and effectively. Continue to listen and learn. Embrace your community and leverage its resources. Expand your network of contacts. Explore new relationships and opportunities. Thinking about ways that you can improve your community and getting involved in community organizations will expand your network of contacts and open up new opportunities. Surround yourself with people who enrich your life, elevate your spirits, and encourage positive action. Avoid negative influences. When I say avoid negative influences, I mean get away from them. It may take time, but removing yourself from people or other negative influences that you believe are holding you back needs to be a primary goal. If you have friends who are negative influences—get away from them and make new friends. Be selective. Don't be seduced by the trappings of consumerism. Make your own luck by being open, flexible, and optimistic. Challenge your assumptions and question your perceptions. Try to see the viewpoints of others—consider perspectives other than your own. Respect all others—especially the elderly and those in positions of authority. Allow compassion and mindfulness to enrich your life as you enrich the lives of others. Be thoughtful, considerate, and generous. Consider your life a work in progress and design it as you would a temple, one carefully laid brick at a time. Don't look for the easy way. Look for the right way—the best way. If you are going to do something, do it right or don't do it at all. Don't settle for less.

With each task you complete, with each challenge you overcome, your competency and commitment will continue to build. With each step forward, you will gain greater strength, increased courage, and a confidence that will attract and inspire others to believe in your potential. Believe in yourself. Know that your potential truly is unlimited. Action is magic. Continue taking action—and discover the magic within you! Change won't happen overnight. It will take time—but it will happen. Stay the course. Enjoy the ride. Have faith in yourself. *You're the one who's going to make it happen, and if you believe that you can, you're right, you can!*

You are living in a truly amazing century, one that will likely witness greater change than any prior generation in human history. That's pretty amazing when you think about it. You're fortunate to be living during such a remarkable time. The opportunities available to every human being alive today are truly extraordinary. The iPhone that you use to post photos on Instagram has more computing power than NASA had in 1969, when it landed men on the moon. From 2011 to 2013, young people just like you used social media to overthrow repressive governments in Tunisia, Egypt, Libya, and Yemen in what came to be known as the Arab Spring.

Mahatma Gandhi said, "You must be the change you want to see in the world." Think about what you can do with the tools available to you. Think about how you can "be the change" you want to see. Think about how you can make your world and your children's world a better place. Life is a remarkable journey. You determine where it leads by the choices that you make. Get the most out of your one and only life. Choose to lead a happy, successful, and meaningful life, and then show the courage, character, and commitment to do what is required to secure that life for yourself and your family. Godspeed!

Bibliography

Note to readers: This Bibliography contains, to the best of my knowledge, the references I used while writing this book, as well as other articles, blogs, and books that may be useful to you in your quest for a happy, successful, and meaningful life.—GJC

Preface

Bolte Taylor, Jill. February 21, 2013. "The Neuroanatomical Transformation of the Teenage Brain: TEDxYouth@Indianapolis." At https://www.youtube.com/watch?v=PzT_SBl31-s.

"Mindfulness." *Wikipedia.* At https://en.wikipedia.org/wiki/Mindfulness.

"10,000 Hours of Practice." WisdomGroup. At http://www.wisdomgroup.com/blog/10000-hours-of-practice.

"Tiger Woods' Daily Schedule–12 Hour." May 25, 2014. Winning Strategies Magazine. At https://www.facebook.com/Winning.Strategies.magazine/posts/523974171058066.

Introduction

AP/USA Today. January 20, 2014. "Study: Nearly Half of Black Men Arrested by Age 23." At http://www.usatoday.com/story/news/nation/2014/01/20/nearly-half-arrested/4669225.

Federal Bureau of Investigation (FBI). 2011. "They Poison Our Streets with Drugs, Violence, and All Manner of Crime." *National Gang Threat Assessment Report.* At https://www.fbi.gov/about-us/investigate/vc_majorthefts/gangs.

Hall, Katy, and Jan Diehm. September 11, 2013. "The Geography of Unintended Pregnancy (INFOGRAPHIC)." HuffingtonPost.com. At http://www.huffingtonpost.com/2013/09/11/unintended-pregnancy-_n_3906668.html.

Marche, Stephen. June/July 2014. "Manifesto of the New Fatherhood: Why Fathers Matter Now More Than Ever Before. A charge." Esquire.com. At http://www.esquire.com/lifestyle/news/a28987/manifesto-of-the-new-fatherhood-0614.

Plato. Nd. Crito. *The Trial and Death of Socrates: Four Dialogues by Plato.* Translated by Benjamin Jowett. Barnes & Noble Publishing, 2004, p. 52. At http://izquotes.com/quote/146439.

Sainato, Michael. August 19, 2015. "Stephen Hawking, Elon Musk, and Bill Gates Warn About Artificial Intelligence." *Observer Opinion*. Observer.com. At http://observer.com/2015/08 /stephen-hawking-elon-musk-and-bill-gates-warn-about-artificial-intelligence.

U.S. Census Bureau. 2015. At www.census.gov/newsroom/press-releases/2015 /cb15-113.html.

Chapter One: The Importance of Reflection and Self-Examination

Beaton, Caroline. September 25, 2015. "Is It Narcissism—Or Just High, Healthy Self-esteem? How Psychology Tests Are Failing Us: The Data behind Millennial Narcissism." *Psychology Today.com*. At https://www .psychologytoday.com/blog/the-gen-y-guide/201509 /is-it-narcissism-or-just-high-healthy-self-esteem.

Booher, Dianna. January 14, 2016. "What Matters Most in Managing Millennials—Communication" *ForbesWoman*. Forbes.com. At http://www.forbes.com /sites/womensmedia/2016/01/14/what-matters-most-in-managing -millennials-communication/#593d92707bca.

Bortz, Daniel. September 4, 2013. "7 Ways Boomers and Millennials Differ at Work." The Fiscal Times.com. At http://www.thefiscaltimes.com /Articles/2013/09/04/7-Ways-Boomers-and-Millennials-Differ-Work.

Brokaw, Tom. 2004. *The Greatest Generation*. New York: Random House.

Evans, Lisa. November 20, 2015. "How Millennials Can Manage Older Generations without Feeling Awkward." Fast Company.com. At http://www .fastcompany.com/3053484/know-it-all /how-millennials-can-manage-older-generations-without-feeling-awkward.

Iny, Danny. January 20, 2016. "3 Reasons Managers Are Afraid to Hire Millennials." Inc.com. At http://www.inc.com/danny-iny/3-reasons -managers-are-afraid-to-hire-millennials.html.

Kirk, Donald. February 12, 2015. "For Korean Air 'Nut Rage' Lady—No Mercy For Being 'Nutrageous." Forbes.com. At http://www.forbes.com/sites /donaldkirk/2015/02/12/korean-air-nut-rage-exec-goes-to-prison-no-mercy -for-nutrageous-behavior/#689f73b6a78b.

Meister, Jeanne C., and Karie Willyerd. May 2010. "Mentoring Millennials." *Harvard Business Review*. At https://hbr.org/2010/05/mentoring-millennials.

"Millennials Infographic." January 2016. Goldman Sachs.com. At http://www.goldmansachs.com/our-thinking/pages/millennials.

Myers, Karen K., and Kamyab Sadaghiani. March 2010. "Millennials in the Workplace: A Communication Perspective on Millennials' Organizational Relationships and Performance. *Journal of Business and Psychology*. At http://www.ncbi.nlm.nih.gov/pmc/articles/PMC2868990.

Pew Research Center. February 24, 2010. "Millennials: Confident. Connected. Open to Change." *Social & Demographic Trends*. Pew Social Trends.org. At http://www.pewsocialtrends.org/2010/02/24 /millennials-confident-connected-open-to-change.

Pew Research Center. March 7, 2014. "Millennials in Adulthood." At http://www.pewsocialtrends.org/2014/03/07/millennials-in-adulthood.

Sainato, Michael. August 19, 2015. "Stephen Hawking, Elon Musk, and Bill Gates Warn about Artificial Intelligence." *Observer Opinion*. Observer.com. At http://observer.com/2015/08 /stephen-hawking-elon-musk-and-bill-gates-warn-about-artificial-intelligence.

Tanenhaus, Sam. August 15, 2014. "The Millennials Are Generation Nice." New York Times.com. At http://www.nytimes.com/2014/08/17/fashion/the -millennials-are-generation-nice.html?_r=0.

Twenge, Jean. May 2, 2012. "Millennials: The Greatest Generation or the Most Narcissistic?" The Atlantic.com. At http://www.theatlantic.com/national/archive/2012/05 /millennials-the-greatest-generation-or-the-most-narcissistic/256638.

U.S. Census Bureau, Population Division. June 2014. "Annual Estimates of the Resident Population by Sex, Single Year of Age, Race, and Hispanic Origin for the United States: April 1, 2010 to July 1, 2013." At http://factfinder.census.gov/faces/tableservices/jsf/pages/productview .xhtml?pid=PEP_2013_PEPALL6N&prodType=table.

U.S. Chamber of Commerce Foundation. Nd. "The Millennial Generation Research Review." At https://www.uschamberfoundation.org /millennial-generation-research-review.

Voogd, Peter. December 22, 2015. "6 Ways to Attract and Retain a Dynamic Millennial Team." Entreprenuer.com. At http://www.entrepreneur.com /article/253605.

Chapter 2: An Early Fork in the Road

AP Wire Report. January 15, 2013. "N.J. Teacher Loses Appeal of Firing for Facebook Post." First Amendment Center. At http://www.firstamendment center.org/n-j-teacher-loses-appeal-of-firing-for-facebook-post.

Bellezza, Silvia, Francesca Gino, and Anat Keinan. "The Surprising Benefits of Nonconformity." March 18, 2014. *MIT Sloan Management Review*. At http://sloanreview.mit.edu/article/ the-surprising-benefits-of-nonconformity.

Gates, Dominic. March 1, 2014. "Boeing Has Big Tax Refund Coming from Uncle Sam—Again." Seattle Times.com. At http://www.seattletimes.com/business /boeing-has-big-tax-refund-coming-from-uncle-sam-mdash-again.

Huffington, Arianna. 2004. *Pigs at the Trough: How Corporate Greed and Political Corruption Are Undermining America*. New York: Three Rivers Press/Random House.

Kovacik, Robert. September 11, 2014. "Two Saugus High School Students Arrested for Posting 'Inappropriate Photos.'" NBC Southern California. NBC Los Angeles.com. At http://www.nbclosangeles.com/news/local /Two-Saugus-High-School-Students-Arrested-for-Posting-Inappropriate -Photos-274855651.html.

Lessig, Lawrence. *Republic, Lost: How Money Corrupts Congress—and a Plan to Stop It*. New York: Twelve Hachette Book Group.

Lil Wayne's Words of Wisdom & the Rise. Mycomeup.com. Ludwing Music. At https://www.youtube.com/watch?v=FXChcUzUFb8.

Rebell, Bobbi. June 28, 2015. "Tattoos May Be Taboo for U.S. Millennials Seeking to Dress for Success." *Reuters.com*. At http://www.reuters.com/article /us-column-rebell-tattoos-idUSKCN0Q21NU20150728.

Sanders, Bernie. June 25, 2015. "Corporate Greed Must End." *Huffpost Politics*. HuffingtonPost.com. At http://www.huffingtonpost.com/rep-bernie -sanders/corporate-greed-must-end_b_7653442.html.

Singer, Michelle. July 23, 2007 (updated). "Under the Influence." *Sixty Minutes*. CBS News.com. At http://www.cbsnews.com/news/under-the-influence.

Sommer, Jeff. November 14, 2015. "A Tax-Cutting Move That Pfizer Can Hardly Resist." New York Times.com. At http://www.nytimes.com/2015/11/15/ your-money/a-tax-cutting-move-that-pfizer-can-hardly-resist.html.

Stoller, Matt. January 1, 2013. "Eight Corporate Subsidies in the Fiscal Cliff Bill: From Goldman Sachs to Disney to NASCAR." Nakedcapitalism.com. At http://www.nakedcapitalism.com/2013/01/eight-corporate-subsidies-in-the -fiscal-cliff-bill-from-goldman-sachs-to-disney-to-nascar.html.

Thiel, Peter, and Masters, Blake. 2014. *Zero to One: Notes on Startups, or How to Build the Future*. New York: Crown Business/Random House.

Chapter 3: What Do You Want to Do With Your One and Only Life?

Alexander, David, Michael Martina, and Dean Yates. "China's Land Reclamation in South China Sea Grows: Pentagon Report." Reuters.com. At http://www.reuters.com/article/us-southchinasea-china-pentagon-idUSKCN0QQ0S920150821.

"The Asteroid Mining Company." Planetary Resources.com. At http://www.planetaryresources.com/#home-intro.

Barra, Mary. February 2, 2015. "Best Advice: Start with Your Passions, Grow Through Hard Work." LinkedIn.com. At https://www.linkedin.com/pulse/best-advice-start-your-passions-grow-through-hard-work-mary-barra.

Bdeir, Ayah. February 2012. "Building Blocks That Blink, Beep and Teach." TED Talks. At http://www.ted.com/talks/ayah_bdeir_building_blocks_that_blink_beep_and_teach.

Frey, Carl Benedikt, and Michael A. Osborne. *The Future of Employment: How Susceptible Are Jobs to Computerisation?* Oxford, UK: Oxford Martin School. At http://www.futuretech.ox.ac.uk/sites/futuretech.ox.ac.uk/files/The_Future_of_Employment_OMS_Working_Paper_1.pdf.

Bieber, Justin. At https://en.wikipedia.org/wiki/Justin_Bieber.

Bridges, Leon. At http://www.leonbridges.com.

Brownlee, Marques. At https://en.wikipedia.org/wiki/Marques_Brownlee.

Callinan, Adam. January 18, 2016. "6 Personality Traits That Are Perfect for Entrepreneurship." Entrepreneur.com. At http://www.entrepreneur.com/article/254902.

Cama, Timothy. December 7, 2015. "Kerry Says He's Looking to the Private Sector to Solve Climate Change." TheHill.com. At http://thehill.com/policy/energy-environment/262314-kerry-private-sector-is-key-in-climate-fight.

"Climate Change: How Do We Know?" NASA Global Climate Change: Vital Signs of the Planet. At http://climate.nasa.gov/evidence.

Colvin, Geoff. July 23, 2015. "Humans Are Underrated: As Technology Becomes More Dominant in the Workplace, Here Are the Three Job Skills That You Need to Thrive." Fortune.com. At http://fortune.com/2015/07/23/humans-are-underrated.

Crispin, Shawn. January 23, 2016. "China Interfering in Vietnam's Politics with Its South China Sea Moves?" The Diplomat.com. At http://thediplomat.com/2016/01/is-china-interfering-in-vietnams-politics-with-its-south-china-sea-moves.

Cutler, Kim-Mai. October 12, 2015. "AngelList to Power the World's Largest Seed Fund with $400M from Chinese Private Equity Firm." TechCrunch.com. At http://techcrunch.com/2015/10/12/angellist-csc/#.dx2de40:5gkZ.

"Dharma." At https://en.wikipedia.org/wiki/Dharma.

Ellis-Petersen, Hannah. December 6, 2014. "Zoella Sugg Online Queen: Followed by Millions but 'Cripplingly Shy.'" *Culture*. The Guardian.com. At http://www.theguardian.com/technology/2014/dec/05/zoella-sugg-internet-queen-fastest-selling-novel-youtube.

"Facebook Reports Fourth Quarter and Full Year 2014 Results." Investorfb.com. At http://investor.fb.com/releasedetail.cfm?ReleaseID=893395.

"Gerrymandering." At https://en.wikipedia.org/wiki/Gerrymandering.

"Google Inc. Announces Fourth Quarter and Fiscal Year 2014 Results." Investor Relations. Google.com. At https://investor.google.com/earnings/2014/Q4_google_earnings.html.

Greenough, John. July 29, 2015. "10 Million Self-Driving Cars Will Be on the Road by 2020." Business Insider.com. At http://www.businessinsider.com/report-10-million-self-driving-cars-will-be-on-the-road-by-2020-2015-5-6.

Greier, Ben. November 13, 2014. "Using 3-D Printing to Make Jet Engines." Fortune.com. At http://fortune.com/2014/11/13/3-d-printing-jet-engines-alcoa.

Heath, Nick. November 2015. "Why AI Could Destroy More Jobs Than It Creates, and How to Save Them." TechRepublic.com. At http://www.techrepublic.com/article/ai-is-destroying-more-jobs-than-it-creates-what-it-means-and-how-we-can-stop-it.

"How the Tesla Model S Is Made." Tesla Motors Part 1 (WIRED). At https://www.youtube.com/watch?v=8_lfxPI5ObM.

Indiegogo: The Largest Global Crowdfunding & Fundraising Site Online. At https://www.indiegogo.com.

Jarre, Jérôme. At https://en.wikipedia.org/wiki/J%C3%A9r%C3%B4me_Jarre.

Jobs, Steve. 2005. "Stanford Commencement Speech." Business Insider.com. At http://www.businessinsider.com/the-full-text-of-steve-jobs-stanford-commencement-speech-2011-10.

Johnson, T. J. "AirDroids: The Start of The Pocket Drone." At https://www.youtube.com/watch?v=nf_h9ZE_7Mk.

Jones, Jeffery M. June 15, 2015. "Confidence in U.S. Institutions Still below Historical Norms." At http://www.gallup.com/poll/183593/confidence-institutions-below-historical-norms.aspx.

Kernel, Brendan I. January 27, 2015. "Silicon Valley Has Lost Its Way: Can Skateboarding Legend Rodney Mullen Help It?" WIRED.com. At http://www.wired.com/2015/01/rodney-mullen.

Keys, Alicia. "Alicia Keys Calls on Paul Ryan to Bring Criminal Justice Reform to a Vote." #cut50. At http://mic.com/articles/134225/alicia-keys-calls-on-paul-ryan-to-bring-criminal-justice-reform-to-a-vote#.CUYRT8wzY.

"Kickstarter: Helping Bring Projects to Life." At https://www.kickstarter.com.

Krogstad, Jens Manuel, and Passel, Jeffrey S. November 19, 2015. "5 Facts about Illegal Immigration in the U.S." Pew Research Center.org. At http://www.pewresearch.org/fact-tank/2015/11/19/5-facts-about-illegal-immigration-in-the-u-s.

Lubin, Gus. July 21, 2001. "Citi's Top Economist Says the Water Market Will Soon Eclipse Oil." Business Insider.com. At http://www.businessinsider.com/willem-buiter-water-2011-7.

Luckey, Palmer. At https://en.wikipedia.org/wiki/Palmer_Luckey.

MacDonald, Kyle. "One Red Paperclip." At https://en.wikipedia.org/wiki/One_red_paperclip.

Momentum Machines. "The Next Industrial Revolution." At http://momentummachines.com.

Moore's Law. At https://en.wikipedia.org/wiki/Moore%27s_law.

PalerLin, Josh. "How Does a Homeless Man Spend $100?" At https://www.youtube.com/watch?v=AUBTAdI7zuY.

Pearce, Kyle. December 13, 2013. "Why You Should Learn to Code (And How to Do It!)." Diygenius.com. At http://www.diygenius.com/learn-to-code-online.

Pearlstein, Steven. January 17, 2014. Review: *The Second Machine Age*, by Erik Brynjolfsson and Andrew McAfee. Washington Post.com At https://www.washingtonpost.com/opinions/review-the-second-machine-age-by-erik-brynjolfsson-and-andrew-mcafee/2014/01/17/ace0611a-718c-11e3-8b3f-b1666705ca3b_story.html.

Pew Research Center. August 16, 2012. "Further Decline in Credibility Ratings for Most News Organizations." At http://www.people-press.org/2012/08/16/further-decline-in-credibility-ratings-for-most-news-organizations.

"Racial Tension and Protests on Campuses across the Country." November 10, 2015. New York Times.com. At http://www.nytimes.com/2015/11/11/us/racial-tension-and-protests-on-campuses-across-the-country.html?_r=0.

Stanton, Brandon. At https://en.wikipedia.org/wiki/Brandon_Stanton.

Vidal, Corey. At https://en.wikipedia.org/wiki/Corey_Vidal.

Williams, Rhiannon. March 12, 2014. "Digital Natives: 25 Internet Success Stories Aged 25 and under." Telegraph.co.uk. At http://www.telegraph.co.uk /technology/internet/10667632/Digital-natives-25-internet-success-stories -aged-25-and-under.html.

Wuske, Melissa. May 27, 2014. "The Gun Debate: What Everyone Needs to Know." At https://www.forewordreviews.com/reviews/the-gun-debate.

Chapter 4: Developing Your Plan of Action

Alanbrooke Diaries, The. Field Marshal Lord Alanbrooke Interviewed by General Sir Brian Horrocks. At https://www.youtube.com/watch?v=Qhx4z4jGroA.

"Employment." United Nations Economic and Social Council. At http://www.un.org/en/ecosoc/about/employment.shtml.

"Employment and Unemployment among Youth Summary." August 18, 2015. Bureau of Labor Statistics. At http://www.bls.gov/news.release/youth.nr0 .htm.

Feloni, Richard. July 28, 2015. "Kevin O'Leary's Best Advice from His 20s." Business Insider.com At http://www.businessinsider.com /kevin-olearys-best-advice-from-his-20s-2015-7.

Khan Academy. At https://www.khanacademy.org.

Knight, Bobby. "Bobby Knight Quotes." BrainyQuote.com. At http://www.brainyquote.com/quotes/authors/b/bobby_knight.html.

Levinson, Conrad Jay, Jeannie Levinson, and Amy Levinson. 2007. *Guerrilla Marketing: Easy and Inexpensive Strategies for Making Big Profits from Your Small Business*. New York: Houghton Mifflin.

Ogilvy, David. 1985. *Ogilvy on Advertising*. New York: Vintage/Random House.

Rosen, Emanuel. 2000. *The Anatomy of Buzz: How to Create Word of Mouth Marketing*. New York: Doubleday Business/Random House.

Chapter 5: Making the Right Choices

Davenport, Barrie. January 20, 2015. "Making Good Choices: 6 Steps to Reclaim Your Personal Power." LiveBoldandBloom.com. At http://liveboldandbloom .com/01/habits/making-good-choices.

Harrell, Ben. December 25, 2009. "Meet Magnus Carlsen, the New King of Chess." TIME.com. At http://content.time.com/time/world /article/0,8599,1948809,00.html.

Ley, Bob, Mike Greenberg, and Jeremy Schaap. "Outside the Lines: Anatomy of a Fix: Interview with Steven 'Headache' Smith." ESPN.com. At https://espn .go.com/page2/tvlistings/show105transcript.html.

Chapter 6: The Meaning and Importance of Character

Crossan, Mary, Jeffrey Gandz, and Gerard Seijts. February 2012. "Developing Leadership Character." Ivey Business Journal.com. At http://iveybusinessjournal.com/publication/developing-leadership-character.

Hereford, Z. "Ten Character Traits Worth Developing." EssentialLifeSkills.com. At http://www.essentiallifeskills.net/charactertraits.html.

"Karma." At https://en.wikipedia.org/wiki/Karma.

King, Martin Luther. August 28, 1963. "I Have a Dream." American Rhetoric.com. At http://www.americanrhetoric.com/speeches/mlkihaveadream.htm.

McKay, Brett, and Kate McKay. June 25, 2013. "What Is Character? Its 3 True Qualities and How to Develop It." The Art of Manliness.com. At http://www.artofmanliness.com/2013/06/25/what-is-character-its-3-true-qualities-and-how-to-develop-it.

Price-Mitchell, Marilyn. May 6, 2011. "Why Character Counts in Education." *Resilience*. RootsofAction.com. At http://www.rootsofaction.com/intelligence-plus-character-the-goal-of-education-part-1.

Shinkman, Paul D. January 21, 2016. "Lawmakers Blast Possible Demotion of David Petraeus." US News.com. At http://www.usnews.com/news/articles/2016-01-21/john-mccain-jack-reed-blast-possible-demotion-of-david-petraeus.

Socrates. Nd. "Regard your good name as the richest jewel. . . ." IZQuotes.com. At http://izquotes.com/quote/287397.

Chapter 7: How to Communicate Effectively

Bolte Taylor, Jill. "The Neuroanatomical Transformation of the Teenage Brain." TEDxYouth@Indianapolis. YouTube.com. At https://www.youtube.com/watch?v=PzT_SBl31-s.

Bolton, Robert. 1979. *People Skills*. New York: Simon & Schuster.

Branson, Richard. May 11, 2015. "My Top 10 Quotes on Communication." At http://www.virgin.com/richard-branson/my-top-10-quotes-on-communication.

DeMers, Jayson. November 10, 2014. "7 Communication Skills Every Entrepreneur Must Master." Entreprener.com. At http://www.entrepreneur.com/article/239446.

Fitzpatrick, Vince. April 26, 2010. "Effective Communication Leads to Understanding." Sans Technology Institute. At http://www.sans.edu/research/management-laboratory/article/fitzpatrick-mgt421.

Foster, Nancy. April 2015. "Good Communication Starts with Listening." Mediate.com. At http://www.mediate.com/articles/foster2.cfm.

Giedd, Jay N. May 19, 2015. "The Amazing Teen Brain." *Scientific American.* At http://www.nature.com/scientificamerican/journal/v312/n6/full/scientificamerican0615-32.html.

Marshall, John. Nd. "To listen well is as powerful a means of communication and influence as to talk well." BrainyQuote. At http://www.brainyquote.com/quotes/quotes/j/johnmarsha170190.html.

McCormack, Mark H. 1984. *What They Don't Teach You at Harvard Business School: Notes from a Street-smart Executive.* Bantam ed., 1986. New York: Bantam Doubleday.

Porges, Stephen W. 2011. *The Polyvagal Theory: Neurophysiological Foundations of Emotions, Attachment, Communication, and Self-regulation.* New York: W. W. Norton & Company.

Robinson, Lawrence, Jeanne Segal, and Melinda Smith. February 2016. "Effective Communication: Improving Communication Skills in Your Work and Personal Relationships." Helpguide.org. At http://www.helpguide.org/articles/relationships/effective-communication.htm.

Shortell, David. November 23, 2014. "Report on Newtown's Adam Lanza Finds Missed Chances." CNN.com. At http://www.cnn.com/2014/11/21/justice/newtown-shooter-adam-lanza-report.

Sollier, Pierre. 2005. *Listening for Wellness: An Introduction to the Tomatis Method.* Walnut Creek, CA: The Mozart Center Press.

Walters, Jamie, and Sarah Fenson. August 1, 2000. "A Crash Course in Communication." Inc.com. At http://www.inc.com/articles/2000/08/20000.html.

Chapter 8: How Committed Are You to Succeeding?

Cagley, Thomas, and Meghan Cagley. September 28, 2013. "Much Ado about Commitment." Infoq.com. At http://www.infoq.com/articles/much-ado-about-commitment.

Carnegie, Andrew. BrainyQuote.com. At http://www.brainyquote.com/quotes/quotes/a/andrewcarn106123.html.

Dougherty, Jim. December 12, 2012. "To Get a Commitment, Make a Commitment." Harvard Business Review.org. At https://hbr.org/2012/12/to-get-a-commitment-make-a-com.

Gordon, Jan. 2001. "Top Ten Truths about Commitment." QualityCoaching.com. At http://www.qualitycoaching.com/Articles/commitment.html.

Hill, Napoleon. [1937]. 2009. *Think and Grow Rich.* www.PacPS.com. Pacific Publishing Studio.

Hill, Napoleon. Nd. *The Habit of Going the Extra Mile.* A film based on *Think and Grow Rich.* YouTube.com. At https://www.youtube.com/watch?v=eH6s1L_k -FE. See also https://www.youtube.com/watch?v=3HMSjfIovJ4.

James, LeBron. 2013. "LeBron James Quotes." Wise Sayingz of All Time. At https://www.facebook.com/WiseSayingzOfAllTime/ posts/520375454660446.

Morgan, Rebecca L. "The Power of Commitment." At http://www.rebeccamorgan .com/articles/misc/misc16.html.

Nair, Sivaprasad. January 23, 2015. "Work Like Hell: The Inspiring Genius, Elon Musk." NextBigWhat.com. At http://www.nextbigwhat.com /elon-musk-quotes-297.

Wax, Dustin. "The Nature of Commitment." Lifehack.org. At http://www.lifehack .org/articles/featured/9856.html.

Chapter 9: Why Courage Is Critical and How to Develop It

Action, Brian. August 3, 2009. "Facebook Turned Me Down." Twitter.com. At https://twitter.com/brianacton/status/3109544383.

Aronson, Brad. 2016. "Famous Failures: 23 Famous Failures to Inspire You." Blog: Inspirational Stories, Good News & a Focus on the Positive. At http://www.bradaronson.com/famous-failures.

Bloch, Hannah. September 2013. "Famous Failures." NationalGeographic.com. At http://ngm.nationalgeographic.com/2013/09/famous-failures/bloch-text.

Churchill, Winston. Nd. "Courage." At http://www.azquotes.com/quote/532132.

Cutler, Zach. November 6, 2014. "Failure Is the Seed of Growth and Success." Entrepreneur.com. At http://www.entrepreneur.com/article/239360.

Edmondson, Amy C. April 2011. "Strategies for Learning from Failure." Harvard Business Review.com. At https://hbr.org/2011/04/ strategies-for-learning-from-failure.

Estrem, Pauline. September 13, 2010. "Why Failure Is Good for Success." Success. com. At http://www.success.com/article/why-failure-is-good-for-success.

Gregoire, Carolyn. September 16, 2013. "The Science of Conquering Your Fears— And Living a More Courageous Life." HuffingtonPost.com. At http://www .huffingtonpost.com/2013/09/15/conquering-fear_n_3909020.html.

Hartford, Tim. 2011. *Adapt: Why Success Always Starts with Failure.* New York: Farrar, Straus and Giroux.

Hereford, Z. "Live a Life of Courage." EssentialLifeSkills.com. At http://www.essentiallifeskills.net/courage.html.

"How Fear of Failure Destroys Success." Lifehack.org. At http://www.lifehack.org /articles/lifehack/how-fear-of-failure-destroys-success.html.

Jordan, Michael. "Michael Jordan Quotes." BrainyQuote.com. At http://www.brainyquote.com/quotes/quotes/m/michaeljor127660.html.

Maroney, Dianne. 2013. *The Imagine Project: Stories of Courage, Hope and Love.* Parker, CO: Yampa Valley Publishing.

NPR Staff. June 19, 2012. "Failure: The F-Word Silicon Valley Loves and Hates." The Spirit of Innovation. NPR. org. At http://www.npr.org/2012/06/19/155005546/ failure-the-f-word-silicon-valley-loves-and-hates.

O'Neill, Therese. April 11, 2014. "11 Incredible Acts of Courage." MentalFloss. com. At http://mentalfloss.com/article/56157/11-incredible-acts-courage.

Parker, Kathleen. October 14, 2011. "How We Succeed by Failing." Washington Post.com. At https://www.washingtonpost.com/opinions/how-we-succeed -by-failing/2011/10/14/gIQAnDgykL_story.html.

Rapp, Sarah. Nd. "Why Success Always Starts with Failure." Review of *Adapt.* 99u. com. At http://99u.com/articles/7072 /why-success-always-starts-with-failure.

Tough, Paul. September 14, 2011. "What If the Secret to Success Is Failure?" New York Times.com. At http://www.nytimes.com/2011/09/18/magazine/what -if-the-secret-to-success-is-failure.html.

Tracy, Brian. Nd. "The Courage to Take Action." From Brian Tracy. 1997. *A Treasury of Achievement.* Wheeling, IL: Nightingale-Conant. Nightingale.com. At www.nightingale.com/articles/the-courage-to-take-action.

Chapter 10: Is Your Attitude an Asset or a Liability?

"Beyond Distrust: How Americans View Their Government." November 23, 2015. Pew Research Center. At http://www.people-press.org/2015/11/23 /beyond-distrust-how-americans-view-their-government.

Bradberry, Travis. January 19, 2016. "Why Attitude Is More Important Than IQ." Forbes.com. At http://www.forbes.com/sites/travisbradberry/2016/01/19 /why-attitude-is-more-important-than-iq/print.

Campbell, Sherrie, February 26, 2015. "10 Surefire Ways a Positive Attitude Increases Success." Entrepreneur.com. At http://www.entrepreneur.com /article/243218.

Harrell, Keith. March 9, 2009. "Why Your Attitude Is Everything." Success.com. At http://www.success.com/article/why-your-attitude-is-everything.

Hill, Napoleon. "Success Through a Positive Mental Attitude." Pocket Books. iBooks. At https://itunes.apple.com/us/book /success-through-positive-mental/id381618319?mt=11.

James, Geoffrey. August 29, 2014. "How an Upbeat Attitude Makes Success Simple." Inc.com. At http://www.inc.com/geoffrey-james/an-upbeat-attitude -makes-success-simple.html.

Juno, Tom. December 18, 2014. "The Age of Exuberance." Esquire.com. At http://www.esquire.com/news-politics/a31132/age-of-exuberance-1214.

Melendez, Eleazar David. February 14, 2013. "Financial Crisis Cost Tops $22 Trillion, GAO Says." At http://www.huffingtonpost.com/2013/02/14 /financial-crisis-cost-gao_n_2687553.html.

Jefferson, Thomas. Nd. "Nothing can stop the man with the right mental attitude from achieving his goal; . . ." Thomas Jefferson Foundation, Inc. At https:// www.monticello.org/site/jefferson /nothing-can-stop-man-right-mental-attitude-quotation.

Oswald, Andrew J., Eugenio Proto, and Daniel Sgroi. February 10, 2014. *Happiness and Productivity.* Warwick, UK: University of Warwick, and Bonn, Germany: IZA Bonn. At http://www2.warwick.ac.uk/fac/soc/economics/staff/eproto /workingpapers/happinessproductivity.pdf.

Peale, Norman Vincent. [1952]. 2003. The Power of Positive Thinking. New York: Prentice–Hall; Touchstone iBooks. At https://itunes.apple.com/us/book /power-positive-thinking/id381728262?mt=11.

Pittman, Aaron, August 17, 2013. "Your Attitude Is the Reason You're Poor." *Entrepreneur.* At http://thenextweb.com/entrepreneur/2013/08/17 /your-attitude-is-the-reason-youre-poor/#gref.

Sasson, Remez. Nd. "The Power of Positive Thinking." SuccessConsciousness.com. At http://www.successconsciousness.com/index_000009.htm.

Wood-Young, Thomas. 2000. *Intuitive Selling.* 2000. Colorado Springs, CO: WY Publishing.

Young, Thomas. 2016. "Everything Starts with Attitude." SalesTrainingPlus. At SalesTrainingPlus.com., http://salestrainingplus.com/sales-marketing -information/sales-and-marketing-articles/57-everything-starts-with-attitude.

Chapter 11: Choosing the Right Career Path

"Finding the Right Career: Choosing or Changing Jobs and Finding Satisfaction at Work." Nd. HelpGuide.org. At http://www.helpguide.org/articles/work -career/finding-the-right-career.htm.

"Jung Typology Test.Ô" Nd. Personality Test Based on Carl Jung's and Isabel Briggs "Myers' typology. HumanMetrics.com. At http://www.humanmetrics .com/cgi-win/jtypes1.htm.

MMDIÔ *Personality Test.* Nd. Team Technology: Online Business Resources. At http://www.teamtechnology.co.uk.

Rasmussen College. 2014. "Career Aptitude Test." Rasmussen.edu. At http://www.rasmussen.edu/resources/aptitude-test.

Chapter 12: How to Negotiate Successfully

Fisher, Roger, and William L. Ury; Bruce Patton, Ed. 1981. *Getting to Yes: Negotiating Agreement Without Giving In*. London and New York: Penguin Books/Random. See also the Harvard Negotiation Project. At http://www .pon.harvard.edu/category/research_projects/harvard-negotiation-project.

"Method of Harvard Principled Negotiation." At https://en.wikipedia.org/wiki /Method_of_Harvard_Principled_Negotiation.

"Dealing Constructively with Intractable Conflicts." 2003–2016. An Online Course. The Beyond Intractability Project, The Conflict Information Consortium, University of Colorado, Boulder. At http://www .beyondintractability.org/educationtraining /dealing-constructively-intractable-conflicts.

Chapter 13: The Profound Influence of Perception

Brand, Stewart. February 2013. "The Dawn of De-extinction. Are You Ready?" TED Talk. At https://www.ted.com/talks/ stewart_brand_the_dawn_of_de_extinction_are_you_ready?language=en.

Chopra, Deepak, Murali Doraiswamy, Rudolph E. Tanzi, and Menas Kafatos. April 27, 2013. "Time to Get Real: The Riddle of Perception." *Huffpost Healthy Living*. Huffington Post.com. At http://www.huffingtonpost.com /deepak-chopra/time-to-get-real-the-riddle-of-perception_b_2760952.html.

De Grey, Aubrey. At https://en.wikipedia.org/wiki/Aubrey_de_Grey.

Sainato, Michael. August 19, 2015. "Stephen Hawking, Elon Musk, and Bill Gates Warn about Artificial Intelligence." *Observer Opinion*. Observer.com. At http://observer.com/2015/08/ stephen-hawking-elon-musk-and-bill-gates-warn-about-artificial-intelligence.

"Solving Humanity's Grand Challenges." Singularity University.org. At http:// singularityu.org.

Chapter 14: The Power of Compassion

DeSteno, David. July 14, 2012. "The Science of Compassion: Compassion Made Easy." *Sunday Review*. New York Times.com. At http://www.nytimes .com/2012/07/15/opinion/sunday/the-science-of-compassion.html.

Seppala, Emma. May/June 2013. "The Compassionate Mind." Association for Psychological Science. At http://www.psychologicalscience.org/index.php /publications/observer/2013/may-june-13/the-compassionate-mind.html.

Seppala, Emma. June 3, 2013. "Compassion: Our First Instinct." Psychology Today. com. At https://www.psychologytoday.com/blog/feeling-it/201306 /compassion-our-first-instinct.

Tenzin, Gyatso. "Compassion and the Individual." His Holiness the 14th Dalai Lama of Tibet. Dalai Lama.com. At http://www.dalailama.com/messages /compassion.

Chapter 15: Embrace Your Community, and It Will Embrace You

Dore, Bhavya. July 17, 2015. "In the World's Largest Muslim Nation, Hindu Epics Survive and Thrive." Quartz India. At http://qz.com/456563 /in-the-worlds-largest-muslim-nation-hindu-epics-survive-and-thrive.

Enayati, Amanda. June 1, 2012. "The Importance of Belonging." CNN.com. At http://www.cnn.com/2012/06/01/health/enayati-importance-of-belonging.

"Five Reasons Why Community Is Important." Nd. Mood Panda Blog. At http:// moodpanda.tumblr.com/post/49460339385 /five-reasons-why-community-is-important.

"Hinduism in Indonesia." Indonesia Investments.com. At http://www.indonesia -investments.com/culture/religion/hinduism/item250.

Lappé, Frances Moore, and Jeffrey Perkins. 2004. *You Have the Power: Choosing Courage in a Culture of Fear*. New York: Jeremy P. Tarcher/Penguin.

"Muslim Population of Indonesia." November 4, 2010. Pew Research Center. At http://www.pewforum.org/2010/11/04/muslim-population-of-indonesia.

"Population of Indonesia." Indonesia Investments.com. At http://www.indonesia -investments.com/culture/population/item67.

Saletta, Lindsey. "The Importance of Collaborating and Fostering Community." The EveryGirl.com. At http://theeverygirl.com /the-importance-of-collaborating-and-fostering-community.

"Why Young People Join Gangs and What You Can Do." Violence Prevention Institute.com. At http://www.violencepreventioninstitute.com/youngpeople .html.

Zamor, Riché C., Sarah Michelson, Alan O'Hare, Frances Moore Lappé, Lisa R. Fortuna, and Shirley Suet-ling Tang. 2005. "What Is Community, and Why Is It Important?" Ikeda Center for Peace, Learning, & Dialogue. Cambridge, MA. At http://www.ikedacenter.org/thinkers-themes/themes/community/what-is-community-responses.

Chapter 16: How to Deal with Authority

Adams-Fuller, Terri. June 19, 2015. "We Can Overcome Our Biases, Racial and Otherwise, by First Becoming Aware of Them." Quartz.com. At http://qz.com/410254/we-can-overcome-our-biases-racial-and-otherwise-by-first-becoming-aware-of-them. An excerpt from the Washington Peace Center's "From Moment to Movement" Series: Conversations on Race in America in collaboration with Howard University. At http://washingtonpeacecenter.org/node/13953.

Anderson, Elijah. August 13, 2014. "What Caused the Ferguson Riot Exists in So Many Other Cities, Too." Washington Post.com. At https://www.washingtonpost.com/posteverything/wp/2014/08/13/what-caused-the-ferguson-riot-exists-in-so-many-other-cities-too.

Bandler, Aaron. November 11, 2015. "The Top 10 False Claims of Racism on Campus." Daily Wire.com. At http://www.dailywire.com/news/1044/top-10-false-claims-racism-campus-aaron-bandle.

Benson, Grant, T. August 9, 2015. "BUSTED: Cops Release Video of State Rep. Who Claimed Mistreatment During Stop." Breaking911.com. At http://breaking911.com/busted-cops-release-video-of-state-rep-who-claimed-mistreatment-during-stop.

"Black Man Claims 'Racist' Treatment by Police, Cop's Body Cam Shows He's a Liar." April 16, 2015. Video. Top Right News.com. At http://toprightnews.com/black-man-claims-racist-treatment-police-cops-body-cam-shows-hes-liar-video.

Blumstein, Alfred. November 25, 2014. "In Assessing Police Racism, Note Racial Disparity in Criminal Activity." New York Times.com. At http://www.nytimes.com/roomfordebate/2014/09/01/black-and-white-and-blue/in-assessing-police-racism-note-racial-disparity-in-criminal-activity.

Bray, Jeff. January, 2016. "Suspects Who Refuse to Identify Themselves." Police Chief Magazine.org. At http://www.policechiefmagazine.org/magazine/index.cfm?fuseaction=display_arch&article_id=1150&issue_id=42007.

"Brown v. Board of Education Re-enactment." United States Courts.gov. At http://www.uscourts.gov/educational-resources/educational-activities/history-brown-v-board-education-re-enactment.

"Civil Rights Act (1964)." Our Documents.gov. At http://www.ourdocuments.gov
/doc.php?flash=true&doc=97.

Craven, Julia. September 30, 2015. "Black Lives Matter Co-Founder Reflects on
the Origins of the Movement." Huffington Post.com. At http://www
.huffingtonpost.com/entry
/black-lives-matter-opal-tometi_us_560c1c59e4b0768127003227.

"Department of Justice Report Regarding the Criminal Investigation into the
Shooting Death of Michael Brown by Ferguson, Missouri, Police Officer
Darren Wilson." March 4, 2015. Justice.gov. At http://www.justice.gov/sites
/default/files/opa/press-releases/attachments/2015/03/04/doj_report_on
_shooting_of_michael_brown_1.pdf.

"Does Today's Young Generation Respect Authority?" Nd. Debate.org. At http://
www.debate.org/opinions/young-generstion-who-do-not-respect-authority

Durgin, Celina, January 20, 2016. "The Myth of Wanton Police Shootings
Collapses under the Weight of Facts." NationalReview.com At http://www
.nationalreview.com/article/429905/police-shootings-december-2015-facts.

Ehrenfreund, Max. March 4, 2015. "17 Disturbing Statistics from the Federal
Report on Ferguson Police." Washington Post.com. At
https://www.washingtonpost.com/news/wonk/wp/2015/03/04/17
-disturbing-statistics-from-the-federal-report-on-ferguson-police.

Failure to Comply. California Codes. CA Vehicle Code Section 2800-2818.
At http://www.leginfo.ca.gov/cgi-bin/displaycode?section=veh&gro
up=02001-03000&file=2800-2818.

Fake Hate Crimes: A Database of Hate Crime Hoaxes in the USA. At
http://www.fakehatecrimes.org.

"Fifteenth Amendment to the United States
Constitution." At https://en.wikipedia.org/wiki/
Fifteenth_Amendment_to_the_United_States_Constitution.

"Fourteenth Amendment to the United States
Constitution." At https://en.wikipedia.org/wiki/
Fourteenth_Amendment_to_the_United_States_Constitution.

Friend, Jared. October 20, 2015. "Seattle's New Crime Analytics Program
Threatens to Perpetuate Racism in Policing." American Civil Liberties Union
of Washington. At https://aclu-wa.org/blog
/seattle-s-new-crime-analytics-program-threatens-perpetuate-racism-policing.

Gallo, Carmine. Talk Like TED: The 9 Public-Speaking Secrets of the World's Top
Minds. 2014. New York: St Martin's Press.

Gann, Carrie. December 19, 2011. "Arrests Increasing for U.S. Youth." ABC News.
com. At http://abcnews.go.com/Health/arrests-increasing-us-youth
/story?id=15180222.

Kapperler, Victor E. January 7, 2014. "A Brief History of Slavery and the Origins of American Policing." Police Studies Online. At http://plsonline.eku.edu /insidelook/brief-history-slavery-and-origins-american-policing.

Lait, Charlotte. January 17, 2014. "Illinois Is in Top 10 for Teen Unemployment." Chicago Reporter.com. At http://chicagoreporter.com /illinois-top-10-teen-unemployment-report.

La Mastra, Salvator J. July 9, 2015. "Police Brutality and Racism or Millennials' Lack of Respect for Authority?" At http://www.theblaze.com/contributions /police-brutality-and-racism-or-millennials-lack-of-respect-for-authority.

Marikar, Sheila. December 20, 2013. "For Millennials, a Generational Divide." New York Times.com. At http://www.nytimes.com/2013/12/22/fashion /Millenials-Millennials-Generation-Y.html.

McCormack, Simon. January 6, 2014. "Nearly Half of Black Males, 40 Percent of White Males Are Arrested by Age 23." Huffington Post.com. At http://www.huffingtonpost.com/2014/01/06/half-of-blacks-arrested -23_n_4549620.html.

Mussmann, Anna. January 23, 2014. "Millennials Think Authority Figures Are Untrustworthy Idiots, and Modern Culture Is to Blame." Federalist.com. At http://thefederalist.com/2014/01/23/millennials-think-authority-figures -are-untrustworthy-idiots-and-modern-culture-is-to-blame.

Neunzig, Robert. December 12, 2014. "My Turn: Problem Lies with Lack of Respect for Law, Authority Rather Than Police, Racial Profiling." Opinion. Gaston Gazette.com. At http://www.gastongazette.com/article/20141212 /Opinion/312129885.

"Police Brutality in the United States." At https://en.wikipedia.org/wiki /Police_brutality_in_the_United_States.

Schneider, Bill. January 15, 2015. "Do Americans Trust Their Cops to Be Fair and Just? New Poll Contains Surprises." Reuters.com. At http://blogs.reuters. com/great-debate/2015/01/15 /one-third-of-americans-believe-police-lie-routinely.

"Thirteenth Amendment to the United States Constitution." At https://wikipedia .org/wiki/Thirteenth_Amendment_to_the_United_States_Constitution.

Voting Rights Act (1965). Our Documents.gov. At http://www.ourdocuments.gov /doc.php?doc=100.

Whitehead, John W. October 7, 2014. "Should We Just Follow Orders? Rules of Engagement for Resisting the Police State." Rutherford Institute.org. At https://www.rutherford.org/publications_resources/john_whiteheads _commentary/should_we_just_follow_orders_rules_of_engagement_for _resisting_the_police_s.

Chapter 17: The Company You Keep

Conley, Mikaela. January 19, 2012. "1 in 5 Americans Suffers from Mental Illness." ABC News.com. At http://abcnews.go.com/blogs /health/2012/01/19/1-in-5-americans-suffer-from-mental-illness.

Cook, Lawrence, and Dana Ford. September 22, 2015. "10 More People Charged in Connection with Hazing Death." CNN.com. At http://www.cnn.com/2015/09/21/us/pi-delta-psi-michael-deng-death.

Deutsch, Gail. July, 16, 2014. "From Best Friends to Killers: Teens Murder Friend Because They 'Didn't Like Her.'" ABC News.com. At http://abcnews.go.com /US/best-friends-killers-teens-murder-friend-didnt/story?id=24573749.

Dicker, Ron. January 24, 2016. "Philip Dhanens, Fresno State Freshman, Dies after Theta Chi Pledge Drinking Party." Huffington Post.com. Video. At http://www.huffingtonpost.com/2012/09/04/frat-boy-dead-after -drink_n_1854811.html.

Mental Disorders in America. Nd. Statistics. Kim Foundation.org. Source: National Institute of Mental Health. At http://www.thekimfoundation.org /html/about_mental_ill/statistics.html.

Rocha, Veronica. July 1, 2015. "Family of Student Who Died in Hazing Incident Sues CSUN, Fraternity." LA Times.com. At http://www.latimes.com/local /lanow/la-me-ln-csun-student-wrongful-death-suit-20150701-story.htm.

Simon, Kate, and Jean-Philippe Delhomme. April 3, 2009. "The Sociopath Next Door." Interview Magazine.com. At http://www.interviewmagazine.com /culture/conscience-lack-of#_.

Hunting Ground, The. 2015. CNN.com. Film clips and information. At http://www.cnn.com/shows/the-hunting-ground.

Chapter 18: The Perils of Consumerism

"Consumerism: Driving Teen Egos—and Buying—through Branding." June 2004. American Psychological Association. At http://www.apa.org/monitor/jun04 /driving.aspx.

Beder, Susan. 1998. "A Community View, Caring for Children in the Media Age." Sydney, AU: New College Institute for Values Research. At https://www.uow.edu.au/~sharonb/children.html.

Gurdon, Meghan Cox. 2004. Book Review. Wall Street Journal. Susan Linn. 2004. Consuming Kids: The Hostile Takeover of Childhood. New York: The New Press. At http://www.consumingkids.com/reviews_interviews/Wall%20 Street%20Journal.htm.

Rose, Jeff. January 23, 2015. "40 Bucks to $10 Million: What Warren Buffett Can Teach You." DailyFinance.com. At http://www.dailyfinance.com/2015/01/23/warren-buffett-coca-cola-story.

"Ten Questions for Mark Cuban." November 2010. Forbes Staff. At http://www.forbes.com/2010/11/03/billionare-mark-cuban-entrepreneur-dallas-mavericks-secrets-self-made-10.html.

Chapter 19: Luck Travels in the Sphere of Efficiency

Bellows, Allan. December 22, 2015. "You Make Your Own Luck." Damn Interesting.com. At http://www.damninteresting.com/you-make-your-own-luck.

Jarrett, Christian. "How to Be Lucky." 99u.com. At http://99u.com/articles/28195/how-to-be-lucky.

Power, Marianne. October 28, 2012, "Feeling Lucky? The Scientific Proof That You DO Make Your Own Luck." MailOnline.co.uk. At http://www.dailymail.co.uk/femail/article-2224473/Feeling-lucky-The-scientific-proof-DO-make-luck.html.

Shenk, Joshua Wolf. 2014. *Powers of Two: Finding the Essence of Innovation in Creative Pairs.* New York: Houghton Mifflin Harcourt.

Webber, Rebecca. May 1, 2010. "Make Your Own Luck: Five Principles for Making the Most of Life's Twists and Turns." Psychology Today.com. At https://www.psychologytoday.com/articles/201005/make-your-own-luck.

Wiseman, Richard. January 9, 2003. "Be Lucky—It's an Easy Skill to Learn." Telegraph.co.uk. At http://www.telegraph.co.uk/technology/3304496/Be-lucky-its-an-easy-skill-to-learn.html.

Wiseman, Richard. 2003. *The Luck Factor: The Four Essential Principles.* New York: Hyperion.

Chapter 20: Respect Your Elders

"How to Respect Your Elders: 8 Steps." Nd. Wiki How to Do Anything. At http://www.wikihow.com/Respect-Your-Elders.

Pujani, Sana. February 15, 2014. "10 Reason Why We Should Respect Our Elders" List Dose.com. At http://listdose.com/10-reason-why-we-should-respect-our-elders.

"7 Cultures That Celebrate Aging and Respect Their Elders." February 25, 2014. Huffington Post.com. At http://www.huffingtonpost.com/2014/02/25/what-other-cultures-can-teach_n_4834228.html.

Confucius. "Filial Piety (Xiao)." 1963. Compiled and translated by Wing-tsit Chan. Analects I:2. In *A Source Book in Chinese Philosophy*. Princeton, NJ: Princeton University Press. See also http://afe.easia.columbia.edu/at/conf_teaching /ct02.html.

Chapter 21: Managing Your Money

Thakor, Manisha; Tom Brakke, Rafael Pardo, Eleanor Blayney, Charles Rotblat, Greg McBride, Michelle Perry Higgins, Rick Ferri, Scott Adams, Michael Kitces, George Papadopoulos, Sheryl Garrett, Larry Zimpleman, and Erin Lantz. April 24, 2013. "The Experts: The Best Financial Advice for Young People Starting Out." Wall Street Journal.com. At http://www.wsj.com /articles/SB10001424127887324474004578442682818178530.

Warren, Elizabeth, and Amelia Warren Tyagi. 2005. *All Your Worth: The Ultimate Lifetime Money Plan*. New York: Simon Schuster/Free Press.

Wheelman, Barbara. "10 Financial Tips for Young People." Bankrate.com. At http://www.bankrate.com/finance/retirement/10-financial-tips-for-young -people-1.aspx.

Chapter 22: Finding Happiness

Becker, Joshua. May 2014. "10 Positive Psychology Studies to Change Your View of Happiness." Becomingminimalist.com. At http://www.becomingminimalist .com/happier.

Brooks, C. Arthur. December 14, 2013. "A Formula for Happiness." December 14, 2013. New York Times.com. At http://www.nytimes.com/2013/12/15 /opinion/sunday/a-formula-for-happiness.html.

Lambert, Craig. March 1, 2001. "The Talent for Aging Well." HarvardMagazine. com. At http://harvardmagazine.com/2001/03 /the-talent-for-aging-wel-html.

Newman, Kira M. July 28, 2015. "Six Ways Happiness Is Good for Your Health." Greater Good. At http://greatergood.berkeley.edu/article/item /six_ways_happiness_is_good_for_your_health.

"9 Tips in Life that Lead to Happiness." Lifehack.com. At http://www.lifehack .org/articles/lifestyle/9-tips-in-life-that-lead-to-happiness.html.

Sasson, Remez. 2002. "Success Consciousness: Attaining Spiritual and Material Success." At http://www.theartofhappiness.net/happiness-resources/free -happiness-ebooks/consciousnessandsuccess.pdf.

Sasson, Remez. Nd. "Don't Let Your Thoughts and Worries Hide Your Happiness." SuccessConsciousness.com. At http://www.successConsciousness.com /happiness-hidden-by-thoughts.html.

Sasson, Remez. Nd. "10 Tips to Start Your Day with Happiness."
    SuccessConsciousness.com. At http://www.successconsciousness.com/blog
    /happiness-fun/10-tips-to-start-your-day-with-happiness.

Sasson, Remez. Nd. "Happiness Is Within Us." SuccessConsciousness.com.
    At http://www.successConsciousness.com/index_00001f.htm.

Shenk, Joshua Wolf. June 2009. "What Makes Us Happy?" The Atlantic.com
    At http://www.theatlantic.com/magazine/archive/2009/06
    /what-makes-us-happy/307439.